T0254972

Lecture Notes
in Business Information Processing 473

LNBIP reports state-of-the-art results in areas related to business information systems and industrial application software development – timely, at a high level, and in both printed and electronic form.

The type of material published includes

- Proceedings (published in time for the respective event)
- Postproceedings (consisting of thoroughly revised and/or extended final papers)
- Other edited monographs (such as, for example, project reports or invited volumes)
- Tutorials (coherently integrated collections of lectures given at advanced courses, seminars, schools, etc.)
- Award-winning or exceptional theses

LNBIP is abstracted/indexed in DBLP, EI and Scopus. LNBIP volumes are also submitted for the inclusion in ISI Proceedings.

Cristine Griffo · Sérgio Guerreiro ·
Maria E. Iacob
Editors

Advances in Enterprise Engineering XVI

12th Enterprise Engineering Working Conference, EEWC 2022
Leusden, The Netherlands, November 2–3, 2022
Revised Selected Papers

 Springer

Editors
Cristine Griffo (iD)
Free University of Bozen-Bolzano
Bolzano, Italy

Sérgio Guerreiro (iD)
Universidade de Lisboa
Lisbon, Portugal

Maria E. Iacob (iD)
University of Twente
Enschede, The Netherlands

ISSN 1865-1348   ISSN 1865-1356 (electronic)
Lecture Notes in Business Information Processing
ISBN 978-3-031-34174-8   ISBN 978-3-031-34175-5 (eBook)
https://doi.org/10.1007/978-3-031-34175-5

This Springer imprint is published by the registered company Springer Nature Switzerland AG
The registered company address is: Gewerbestrasse 11, 6330 Cham, Switzerland

Preface

This book contains the revised papers of the 12th Enterprise Engineering Working Conference, EEWC 2022, held in Leusden, the Netherlands, on November 2–3, 2022. It was organized by the CIAO! Enterprise Engineering Network (CEEN), a community of academics and practitioners who strive to contribute to the development of The Discipline of Enterprise Engineering (EE), and to apply it in practice. The aim is to develop a holistic and general systems theory-based understanding on how to (re)design and run enterprises effectively. The purpose is to develop a consistent and coherent set of theories, models, and associated methods that enable enterprises to reflect, in a systematic way, on how to realize improvements and assist them, in practice, in achieving their aspirations.

In doing so, sound empirical and scientific foundations should underlie all efforts and all organizational aspects that are relevant should be considered, while combining already existing knowledge from the scientific fields of information systems, software engineering, and management, as well as philosophy, semiotics, and sociology, among others. In other words, the (re)design of an enterprise and the subsequent implementation of changes should be the consequence of rational decisions that take into account the nature and reality of the enterprise and its environment, and respect relevant empirical and scientific principles.

Enterprises are considered as systems whose reality has a dual nature by being simultaneously, on the one hand, centrally and purposefully (re)designed, and, on the other hand, emergent in a distributed way, given the fact that their main agents, the humans that are the "pearls" of the organization, act with free will in a creative and in a responsible (or sometimes not) way. We acknowledge that, in practice, the development of enterprises is not always a purely rational/evidence-based process. As such, we believe the field of EE aims to provide evidence-based insights into the design and evolution of enterprises and the consequences of different choices irrespective of the way decisions are made.

The origin of the scientific foundations of our present body of knowledge is the CIAO! Paradigm (Communication, Information, Action, Organization) as expressed in our Enterprise Engineering Manifesto and the paper: "The Discipline of Enterprise Engineering". In this paradigm, organization is considered to emerge in human communication, through the intermediate roles of information and action. Based on the CIAO! Paradigm, several theories have been proposed, and are still being developed. They are published as technical reports.

CEEN welcomes proposals of improvements to our current body of knowledge, as well as the inclusion of compliant and alternative views, always keeping in mind the need to maintain global systemic coherence, consistency, and scientific rigor of the entire EE body of knowledge as a prerequisite for the consolidation of this new engineering discipline. Yearly events like the Enterprise Engineering Working Conference and associated Doctoral Consortium are organized to promote the presentation of EE research and application in practice, as well as discussions on the contents and current state of our body of theories and methods.

Since 2005, CEEN has organized the CIAO! Workshop and, since 2008, its proceedings have been published as *Advances in Enterprise Engineering* in the Springer LNBIP series. From 2011 onwards, this workshop was replaced by the Enterprise Engineering Working Conference (EEWC). The EEWC 2022 edition was the first in-person edition after the Covid-19 pandemic. The works presented were widely debated, which resulted in a deepening of the written works presented in these proceedings. Additionally, the merger of CEEN, EE-Network.eu and the Enterprise Engineering Institute into an integrated network, which had already yielded good results in the 2021 edition, was consolidated with the 2022 edition.

This volume contains the proceedings of EEWC 2022, which received 13 submissions. In pursuit of the spirit of being a working conference, it is now the norm of EEWC to publish post-proceedings after the event, where the papers that are presented are made available to conference participants, and are revised and extended by the authors taking into account the discussions that happened at the conference, the feedback of the reviewers and new developments that might have taken place in the research during/after the conference. So each submission was reviewed (double-blind) by three members of the Program Committee (PC) and, based on the reviews, the PC-chairs decided to accept for presentation and publication a total of 6 papers, 2 as full and 4 as short, with the possibility, communicated to the authors, of the best 2 short papers being promoted to full papers in the final proceedings. After the conference presentations, authors were given the opportunity to improve their papers according to the reviewer's feedback and discussions at the conference and submit an extended new version of the paper, together with a changes report. Papers were then the subject of a second review round by the PC-chairs, with input, as needed, from the PC members that originally reviewed the paper. After the second review round, the PC-chairs decided to promote 2 short papers to full, so the final decision was to accept 4 papers as full and 2 as short. This year's edition featured two keynotes, by Jaap Gordijn and Adina Aldea, who were invited to publish their work in these proceedings as invited papers.

EEWC aims to address the challenges that modern and complex enterprises are facing in a rapidly changing world. The participants of the working conference share a belief that dealing with these challenges requires rigorous and scientific solutions, focusing on the design and engineering of enterprises. The goal of EEWC is to stimulate interaction between the different stakeholders, scientists, and practitioners interested in making enterprise engineering a reality.

We thank all the participants, authors, and reviewers for their contributions to EEWC 2022 and hope that you find these proceedings useful to your explorations on current enterprise engineering challenges.

April 2023   Cristine Griffo
                                                                            Sérgio Guerreiro
                                                                            Maria E. Iacob

Organization

Program Chairs

Cristine Griffo   Free University of Bozen-Bolzano, Italy
Sérgio Guerreiro   Universidade de Lisboa, Portugal
Maria E. Iacob   University of Twente, The Netherlands

Program Committee

Alberto Silva   University of Lisboa, Portugal
Bas Vangils   Strategy Alliance, The Netherlands
David Aveiro   University of Madeira, Portugal
Eduard Babkin   Higher School of Economics, Russia
Erik Proper   TU Wien, Austria
Graham McLeod   Inspired.org, South Africa
Hans Mulder   University of Antwerp, Belgium
Jaap Gordijn   Vrije Universiteit Amsterdam, The Netherlands
Jan Verelst   University of Antwerp, Belgium
Jens Gulden   Universität Duisburg-Essen, Germany
Joseph Barjis   San José State University, USA
Marcello Bax   Federal University of Minas Gerais, Brazil
Maria da Silva Teixeira   Federal University of Espírito Santo, Brazil
Maria-Eugenia Iacob   University of Twente, The Netherlands
Marien Krouwel   University of Maastricht, The Netherlands
Mark Mulder   Enterprise Engineering Institute, The Netherlands
Martin Op 't Land   Capgemini, The Netherlands
Mauricio Almeida   Federal University of Minas Gerais, Brazil
Miguel Mira da Silva   Universidade de Lisboa, Portugal
Monika Kaczmarek   University of Duisburg-Essen, Germany
Niek Pluijmert   INQA Quality Consultants BV, The Netherlands
Pascal Ravesteijn   HU University of Applied Sciences Utrecht,
                               The Netherlands
Peter Loos   Saarland University, Germany
Petr Kremen   Czech Technical Univ. in Prague, Czech Republic
Robert Pergl   Czech Technical Univ. in Prague, Czech Republic
Stephan Aier   University of St. Gallen, Switzerland

Stijn Hoppenbrouwers   HAN University of Applied Sciences,
                                  The Netherlands
Tatiana Poletaeva   Higher School of Economics - Nizhny Novgorod,
                                  Russia

Contents

Invited Papers from Keynote Presentations

The Business Model of Digital Ecosystems: Why and How You Should Do It

Jaap Gordijn[1,2]([✉]) [iD] and Roel Wieringa[2]

[1] VU Amsterdam, De Boelelaan 1111, 1081 HV Amsterdam, The Netherlands
j.gordijn@vu.nl
[2] The Value Engineers, Soest, The Netherlands
{jaap,roel}@thevalueengineers.nl

Abstract. Digital ecosystems and platforms require a business model, which is a model of how a business creates, delivers, and captures value. We argue that the business model should be a *networked* business model, as ecosystems and platforms are connected networks of organizations and consumers. Furthermore, we emphasize that a business model should be a *conceptual* model that is expressed using a (semi) formal language. This is not only needed in order to create an unambiguous and shared understanding of the ecosystem at hand; it is also a prerequisite for software-assisted analysis and for the use of other design techniques, e.g. for business process engineering, and ICT architecture design. We explain these two requirements concerning business modelling using a series of industry strength cases.

Keywords: digital ecosystem · platform · e^3value · network · conceptual model

1 Introduction

The notions of 'business model' and 'digital ecosystem' are closely related: Every network of actors requires a way to be financial sustainable on the long term for all actors involved. However, the idea of 'business model' is understood in very different ways: In the field of business development, a business model refers to how parties can earn money, hence the focus is on the 'business' first. In Computer Science, the emphasizes is more on the *conceptual model*, which is a formalization of the ecosystem at hand, usually with the aim to create a shared understanding and to enable (automated) analysis.

In this paper, we argue that a business model should consider the *network* as a first class citizen. Each business model contains at least two actors: A buyer and a seller, and hence it can be considered as a network. However, in reality, both digital ecosystems and platform, and so their business models, are far more complicated, as they contain many more actors than just two. This already holds for centrally led platforms, such as Meta, Alphabet, Amazon, and Netflix, which are all conglomerates of a large number of parties. Moreover, there are also ecosystems that are physically organized as networks of actors by their nature: For example the electricity network, telecommunication, railway, and

C. Griffo et al. (Eds.): EEWC 2022, LNBIP 473, pp. 3–16, 2023.
https://doi.org/10.1007/978-3-031-34175-5_1

international clearing of intellectual property rights on music all have a strong network orientation.

This paper is structured as follows. In Sect. 2, we first introduce the notions of 'ecosystem' and 'platform'. Thereafter (Sect. 3), we define the concept of 'business model' and we discuss two different techniques for representing a business model, namely the Business Model Canvas and e^3value. We explain both techniques briefly using the same example, namely AirBnb. Then we discuss two requirements regarding business models of digital ecosystems. First, in Sect. 4 we argue that in a business model of digital ecosystem, the network should be the first class citizen. Second, we claim that business models should be *conceptual* models, to allow for creation of shared understanding and further software-assisted analysis (Sect. 5). Finally, Sect. 6 presents our conclusions.

2   Ecosystems and Platforms

In our upcoming book about digital business ecosystems [12], we define the notion of ecosystem as follows: 'A business ecosystem is a system of economic actors that depend on each other for their survival and well-being'. This definition is based on the analysis of the biological ecosystem concept by [13]. The biological ecosystem metaphor was actively introduced by [7,8] and later used actively by [3,4].

There are number of remarks in place regarding this definition. First, a business ecosystem consists of many *economic* actors (meaning entities who decide themselves to do economic transactions or not) who form a *network*, where the actors are the nodes, and the economic value transfers are the edges. Second, in a business ecosystem, actors have a *dependency* relation with each other. This means that if an actor defaults, on the longer term the whole network default, provided that no counter measures are taken.

In reality, all economic activity takes place in a business ecosystem; already if there is one buyer and one seller, there is a business ecosystem. Consequently, the list of examples is endless. However, some ecosystems emphasize the networked idea more than others. For example, energy networks, the Internet, railways, and postal services are networked in terms of their production- and delivery processes, and often also in terms of the transfer of economic value transfers.

However, there are also business ecosystems where one specific actor plays a very dominant role. Although perhaps suggested differently by the recent big US-tech firms, such centralized ecosystems already exist for a long time. A *platform* is a shared infrastructure of a value network on top of which members of the value network create additional value [12]. Although not all platforms have a dominant actor (a counter example is OpenBazaar, which is a full decentralized trading platform), many platforms are centrally operated and led. Examples are Facebook, Twitter, NetFlix, Google, Spotify, Amazon and many other companies whose ambition it is to create a centralized, dominated platform. Therefore, if we speak about platforms, very often this refers to *centralized* platforms. Platforms have an *infrastructural* aspects, meaning that they provide products and/or services that are shared by other services. The latter service create *additional* products or services, *on top of* the infrastructural services or products. Android is a platform operated by Google, and others (Facebook, LinkedIn and not in the least Google itself) provide value added services on top of it.

3 Business Models

3.1 Definition

Ecosystems and platforms require a *business model*. Over the past years, the notion of 'model' as part of the concept of 'business model' has received an own interpretation, which is not the same as 'model' in the conceptual modeling field. In the latter, 'model' refers to the idea that, for some reasons, it is useful to develop an abstraction of reality. Reasons to do is to create a clear, well understood, and agreed set of requirements that can be the starting point to develop an information system. Conceptual modeling comes with notations, techniques and methods to produce the models, that are rather formal and leave no room for different interpretations. The notion 'business model' is more loosely defined; it is about how money is earned. Business models are often expressed very informally, even by means of unstructured natural text. This results unavoidably in many interpretations by different stakeholders. Clearly, the focus is more on 'business' than on 'model'.

We define 'business model' differently: 'A business model is a *conceptual model* of how a business creates, delivers, and captures value' [12]. As in our view, business models are always networks, multiple actors are involved. In our interpretation, the idea of 'conceptual model' is very important. We argue that a business model should be (re)*designed*, just as an engineer designs a bridge or an electronics circuit. For designing a business model, a language to express the business model (e.g. e^3value), and tools to analyze the business model (e.g. discounted cash flow analysis, fraud assessment, sensitivity analysis) are needed. In other words, we extend the idea of conceptual modeling, which is well known and successful in the Computer Science discipline, to the business domain.

We also argue that a business model is about an *ecosystem* (or a platform as a special case) and is not restricted to *single focal* enterprise and its direct environment. This is because a business model as strong as its weakest actor; in other words, if some actor goes out of business after a while, the whole ecosystem is affected.

3.2 Techniques

There are many techniques to express a business model. We discuss two of them: The Business Model Canvas (BMC) [10] and e^3value [1]. Figure 1 represents the business model of AirBnb as a BMC. Because AirBnb is an example of a centralized platform, the business model is actually about the *focal actor* AirBnB. A BMC consists of nine blocks (key partners, key activities, value proposition, customer relationships, customer segments, cost structure, and revenue streams), and illustrates the focal actor AirBnb and its direct environment in terms of partners (including suppliers) and customers. Although the importance and acceptance of the BMC by the industry is impressive, there are a number of shortcomings. First of all, the formalization is weak as it only consists of nine boxes. This makes it difficult to analyse and evaluate a BMC with software tools. At the same time, the BMC simplicity is likely its strongest point: it not difficult to understand what is meant by the nine boxes, so the BMC is easy to learn and apply. Secondly, the BMC ignores the *network* aspect, as it takes a focal actor and its environment only.

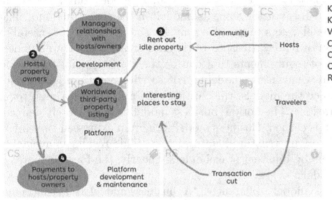

KP: Key partners
KA: Key activities
VP: Value proposition
CR: Customer relationships
CS1: Customer segments
CS2: Cost structure
RS: Revenue streams

Source: Strategyzer website

Fig. 1. AirBnb expressed as a BMC

Figure 2 models the same case, namely AirBnb as an e^3value model. There is no focal actor; all actors are equally important. The e^3value shows the primary value transfers (stay for money), and the secondary value transfers that facilitate that stay (specification of stay, list of possible stays, reservation, money). From the model can be seen that AirBnb earns money by offering reservations. Additionally, the model shows how we model mediation in e^3value: the primary transfer (stay for money) is triggered by the customer need of the visitor (stay) and is independent from AirBnb. However, mediation is modeled as a case of *matching*, where the visitor and a host both have a need, namely 'stay' and 'visitor' respectively. These needs are matched by AirBnb. Finally, the model shows an additional actor, namely a financial service provider (Paypal). The model is more complex than the corresponding BMC. The expressive power of e^3value is higher than the BMC, but e^3value is more difficult to learn and apply correctly. The same holds for the level of formality; because e^3value models are a formalization of a business model, it allows for automated analysis tools, such as economic value flow analysis and fraud assessment [5]. Finally, the e^3value model shows the network, and could easily be extended with other actors such as handyman, energy providers, etc.

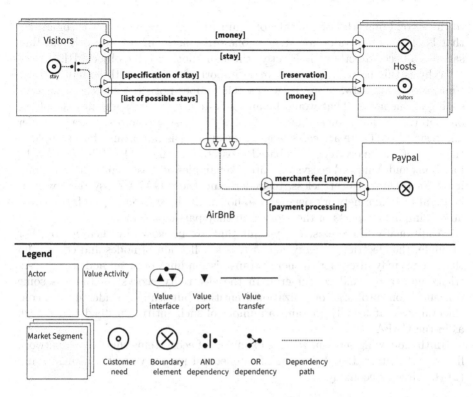

Fig. 2. AirBnb expressed as an e^3value model

4 Digital Ecosystems: Consider the Network as First Class Citizen

This paper is about two requirements concerning the business model of a digital ecosystem: (1) a business model should have a network orientation instead of a single/focal actor perspective, and (2) a business model should be a *conceptual* model. We will elaborate these requirements in this section and the next section.

Our interpretation of 'network' is following: 'A network consists of nodes and edges between nodes' (following the definition of a *Graph* in Computer Science). Nodes and edges are generic constructs that may refer the nearly everything. In our case, the understanding is more restricted: A node actor is an entity that is responsible for its survival and well-being [1]. The edges are value transfers, which express the willingness of two actors to transfer a value object from the first to the second one [1]. For the sake of completeness, a value object is something that is of economic value for at least one other actor in the network and that satisfies a need directly or indirectly (through another value object) [1].

Why is this network perspective so important? We give three motivations. First, ecosystems always *are* networks. There does not exist an ecosystem consisting of one actor. That would be an ecosystem that exists for the sake of the one actor, and that is meaningless. There are at least two actors, e.g. a customer and a supplier. There are cases where a focal actor is important, for example in the case of the many tech-firm based ecosystems. The GAFA (Google, Apple, Facebook and Amazon) ecosystems are all examples of ecosystems with one dominant focal actor. Nevertheless, to understand these GAFA ecosystems well, it is useful to take a network perspective, not in the least because the focal actors absorb important parts of the ecosystem they participate in.

Additionally, there exist ecosystems that are networks by their *nature*. For example, the electricity energy *network*, is a collection of nodes and edges, and these edges may also refer to energy transmission lines between nodes (e.g. electricity generators and consumers). In the electricity ecosystem there is some concentration into large organizational entities, but while considered on a continental scale, it usually contains a number of such entities, instead of one such as in the GAFA case.

In the following section, we give examples of ecosystems that have a network flavour: (1) international clearing of intellectual property rights on music, and (2) the circular economy.

4.1   International Clearing of Intellectual Property Rights on Music

Figure 3 gives a compact e^3value model of international clearing of intellectual property rights on music, specifically the Public Performance Right (PPR) (see for more information about the case [2]). If users play music in a public venue, e.g. a restaurant, they need to pay to collecting societies for doing so. These collecting societies collect fees for the parties they represent, e.g. the artists and producers. Note that in this paper, we only focus on clearing rights on recordings; there are other rights, such as the author rights on works, that we do not consider.

A collecting society pays money to right holders based on the recordings played. In Fig. 3, an envisioned future scenario is represented, namely that restaurants pay for each recording they play (referred to as pay-per-play). A recording has multiple right holders, in this model of two classes, namely artists and producers. The AND dependency represents that right holders of both classes are paid. Typically, per class, there are multiple right holders on a recording, here we assume four artists and two producers.

The e^3value model in Fig. 3 has a specific feature, namely a market segment (collecting society), which exchanges objects of value with itself (both annotated with #1). A collecting society pays directly an artist (this happens if the collecting society clears the rights for that artist), *or* pays to an another collecting society (who operates on behalf of that actor), who in turn pays that specific artist. The same holds for producers. Note that in e^3value, value transfers with the same actor are forbidden, as it makes no sense to sell products or services to itself. There is however one exception to the rule, namely if value transfers (directly of indirectly) connect to the *same* market segment, as is the case in Fig. 3. In this specific instance, the transfer between the same market segment means: *select another actor in the market segment to exchange value objects with*. Since market segments are sets of actors, at the actor level there are only transfers between *different* actors.

It is obvious that this IPR case has a clear network orientation, as *national* collecting societies operate in a network to clear *international* property rights.

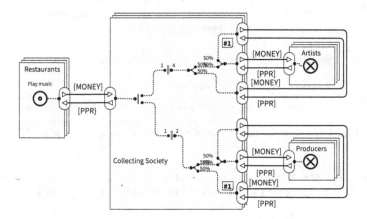

Fig. 3. International clearing of intellectual property rights on music expressed as e^3value model

4.2   The Circular Economy

A special case of a networked ecosystem is a circular ecosystem. Figure 4 presents an anonymized version of such an ecosystem. In brief, the company 'Widget Engineers' build widgets and uses components to do so. If the 'Widget Engineers' creates a widget, a disposal fee is paid to the 'Disposal Fee Foundation', in return for compliance with a national that prescribes. Once the widget is end-of-life, the 'Disposal Fee Foundation' pays a logistic provider to transport the widget from the customer to the 'Disassembler'. The 'Disposal Fee Foundation' also pays a fee to the 'Disassembler', who breaks the widget into raw materials again, which are sold the component supplier. Circularity can be seen due to the subsidizing scheme, and that pieces of the widget are broken down into raw materials, which are used to manufacture new widgets. We argue that to understand a circular business model, understanding of the network is critical.

Finally, focus on the network can be motivated to design ecosystems where (decision) power is fairly distributed, to avoid emergence of GAFA like companies.

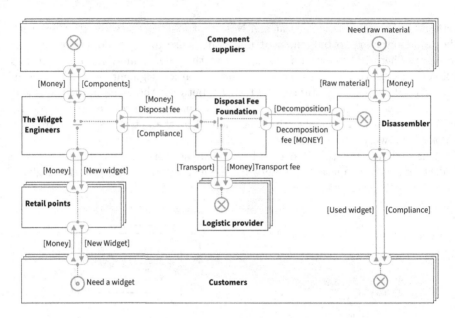

Fig. 4. A circular economy ecosystem expressed as $e^3 value$ model

We argue that if checks and balances are properly designed in a network of stake-holders, it is more difficult to take over and monopolize that network.

5   Digital Ecosystems: Conceptual Modeling

The notion of 'model' in 'business model' is usually not very well defined, but can be seen as some abstraction from reality, focusing on the essentials of businesses. We argue that a business model should be seen as a *conceptual* model. Conceptual modelling is the activity of formally describing some aspects of the physical and social world around us for purposes of understanding and communication [9].

There are a number of reasons why a (semi) formal description of reality is important, one of them a precise and shared understanding of that reality by all stakeholders involved. As an ecosystem implies a multi-stakeholder effort by definition creating such understanding is far from trivial. Conceptual models are then a required addition to text-only descriptions of the ecosystem at hand. However, in this paper, we want to put forward a second argument for the formalization of business models, and that is software-assisted analysis. We discuss three examples of this.

5.1   Net Value Flow Analysis

If an $e^3 value$ model is properly quantified, the model can be used to derive *value flow* sheets (see Table 1 for an example). Figure 5 shows an $e^3 value$ model where

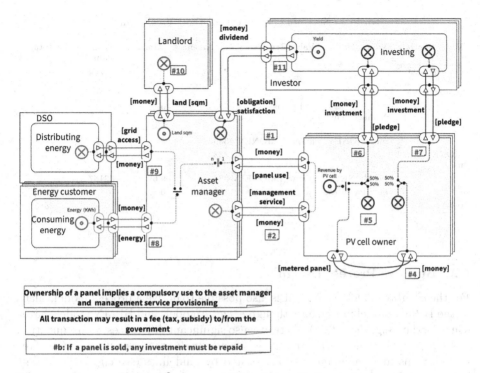

Fig. 5. $e^3 value$ model for photo-voltaic panels

people own, sell, and buy photo-voltaic cells. These cells are physically hosted by an asset manager, in a solar farm. The asset manager rents land from a land manager, often a farmer. Generated energy is sold to customers.

Table 1 shows the incoming value flows (money for use of the panel) and outgoing money flows (management service for money) for the green value path. If the $e^3 value$ is property quantified (e.g. the number of customer needs, the number of customers, and the pricing formulas for the money flows), such a value flow sheet can be automatically generated by the software tooling. This also allows to change parts of the quantification and to quickly see the effects (we call this sensitivity analysis).

Table 1. Net value flow sheet for the PV cell owner

Value Interface	Value Port	Value Transfer	Occurrences	Valuation	Economic Value	Total
Management ser- vice,MONEY			3333		−3333	
	in: Management service	(all transfers)	3333	0	0	
	out: MONEY	[money]:MONEY	3333	1	−3333	
MONEY,Panel use			3333		32167	
	in: MONEY	[money]:MONEY	33333	9.65	32167	
	out: Panel use	(all transfers)	3333	0	0	
total for actor						28833

5.2   Business Process Design

For the e^3value model in Fig. 5, it is also possible to derive a process model, such as the BPMN model in Fig. 6. Although e^3value models and BPMN models have some overlap (e.g. the actors), there are also significant differences. Consequently, it is not possible to derive BPMN models from e^3value models automatically. We consider this more as manual task, assisted by guidelines (see e.g. [11]). More- over, a BPMN model usually exposes more operational details than the associ- ated e^3value model. This is because the BPMN model shows how the e^3value is put into operation, e.g. how value transfers as stated in an e^3value are actually performed. Also, an e^3value model does not show a control flow, e.g. the time ordering of the value transfers, whereas a BPMN modes. This adds an additional level of detail, which can not be derived from the e^3value model.

5.3   Fraud Analysis

Another analysis possibility is fraud analysis. Normally, an e^3value describes an *ideal* world, that is a world where everyone behaves as specified by the e^3value model. An important construct is the value interface, which prescribes that *all* value ports in a value interface exchange an object of value, or *none* at all. For example, in Fig. 7, if user A buys a subscription s/he always pays for it, and vice versa. In case of business development, it is already sufficiently difficult to understand what happens if everyone behaves honestly, rather than to assume that someone may commit a fraud.

However, in reality, people commit frauds, e.g. behave in a *sub-ideal* way. For example, some value object may not be transferred at all, or may be damaged or the wrong one. Also, some value transfers may happen that are hidden for some parties in the e^3value model. Finally, parties may collude to commit a fraud (see e.g. [5,6]).

In Fig. 7 [5], a sub-ideal model is shown, which is known as revenue-sharing fraud. In brief, the revenue-sharing fraud works as follows. First, the subscription

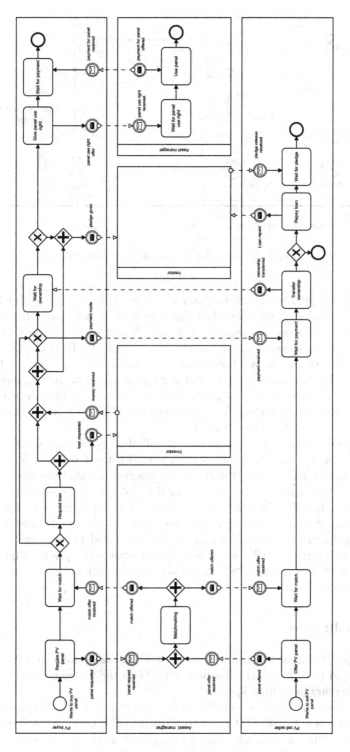

Fig. 6. BPMN model for photo-voltaic panels

14   J. Gordijn and R. Wieringa

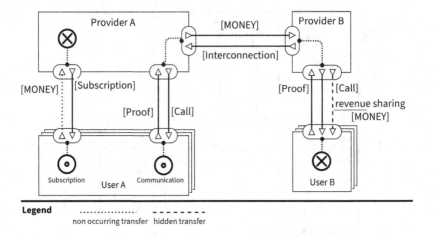

Fig. 7. Fraud in telecommunication networks

of user A is not paid for, hence the money flow is a *non-occurring* value transfer. There are several ways to accomplish this, which we do not elaborate further on. Now, suppose that user A wants to call user B, and user A has a subscription at provider A, and user B has a subscription at provider B. If user A wants to set up a call with user B, two telecommunication providers are needed. Provider A receives the call from user A, and asks provider B to interconnect, since provider B hosts user B. In telecommunication terminology, this service is called interconnection, and provider A pays provider B a fee for that service. Finally, provider B delivers the call to user B.

The fraud is that user A and user B collude, e.g. in reality are the same person. If user A calls user B many times, user B can ask provider for a revenue sharing deal, e.g. receiving part of the interconnection fee that provider B obtains from provider A. This revenue sharing deal is not visible for provider A, hence it is a hidden transfer. Moreover, because user A found a way not to pay for its subscription, provider A pays for this fraud only, via the interconnection fee.

The model in Fig. 7 can be automatically generated via software tooling [5] that uses as input an ideal e^3value model, and trust assumptions. The software tool uses heuristics about fraud, and is able to rank frauds, e.g. based on their impact on the victim.

6   Conclusions

In this paper, we argued by using a series of real life case studies that the business model should (1) consider the business *network* as the first class citizen, and (2) use a *conceptual* modelling approach.

Concerning the emphasis on the network, we observe that each ecosystem or platform is a network, as it minimally consists of a consumer and a supplier, exchanging things of economic value with each other. However, most ecosystems and platforms in practice are far more complicated than just two parties. This holds for the well-known big-tech platforms, but also for ecosystems where the (physical) network plays an important role. Examples include the electricity network, circular economy networks, and international clearing of intellectual property rights.

We also claim that business modelling is about *conceptual* modelling. The first argument is that for business development, a precise and shared understanding of the ecosystem or platform is needed. Creating an unambiguous and common representation is exactly the goal of conceptual modelling. Furthermore, (semi) formalization paves the way for automated analysis, e.g. net cash flow analysis and fraud analysis. Moreover, it can be used as point of departure for business process engineering, and the design of an ICT architecture.

Acknowledgements. This work is part of the Horizon Europe project Music360. The project Music360 has received funding from the European Union's Horizon Europe research and innovation programme under grant agreement No. 101094872.

References

1. Gordijn, J., Wieringa, R.: E3value User Guide - Designing Your Ecosystem in a Digital World, 1st edn. The Value Engineers (2021)
2. Hotie, F., Gordijn, J.: Value-based process model design. Bus. Inf. Syst. Eng. **61**, 163–180 (2017)
3. Iansiti, M., Levien, R.: The Keystone Advantage: What the New Dynamics of Business Ecosystems Mean for Strategy, Innovation, and Sustainability, vol. 3. Harvard Business School Press, United States (2004)
4. Iansiti, M., Levien, R.: Strategy as ecology. Harvard Bus. Rev. **82**(3) (2004)
5. Ionita, D., Wieringa, R., Gordijn, J., Yesuf, A.S.: Quantitative, value-driven risk analysis of e-services. J. Inf. Syst. **33**(3), 45–60 (2019). https://doi.org/10.2308/isys-52150
6. Kartseva, V., Gordijn, J., Tan, Y.-H.: Designing value-based inter-organizational controls using patterns. In: Lyytinen, K., Loucopoulos, P., Mylopoulos, J., Robinson, B. (eds.) Design Requirements Engineering: A Ten-Year Perspective. LNBIP, vol. 14, pp. 276–301. Springer, Heidelberg (2009). https://doi.org/10.1007/978-3-540-92966-6_16
7. Moore, J.F.: Predators and prey: a new ecology of competition. Harv. Bus. Rev. **71**(3), 75–75 (1993)
8. Moore, J.F.: The Death of Competition: Leadership and Strategy in the Age of Business Ecosystems. HarperBusiness (1996)
9. Mylopoulos, J.: Conceptual modeling and telos, chap. 2. In: Loucopoulos, P., Zicari, R. (eds.) Conceptual Modeling, Databases, and CASE: An Integrated View of Information Systems Development, pp. 201–213. McGraw Hill, NY (1992)
10. Osterwalder, A., Pigneur, Y.: Business Model Generation: A Handbook for Visionaries, Game Changers, and Challengers. The Strategyzer Series. Wiley (2010)
11. Torres, I., Fantinato, M., Branco, G., Gordijn, J.: Software and systems modeling guidelines to derive an e3value business model from a BPMN process model: an experiment on real-world scenarios. Software and Systems Modeling (2023). https://doi.org/10.1007/s10270-022-01074-1. https://dise-lab.nl/wp-content/uploads/2023/02/Isaac-SandS2023.pdf

12. Wieringa, R., Gordijn, J.: Digital Business Ecosystems - How to Create, Capture, and Deliver Value in Business Networks. The Value Engineers (2023, forthcoming)
13. Willis, A.J.: The ecosystem: an evolving concept viewed historically. Funct. Ecol. **11**(2), 268–271 (1997)

Current Challenges and Opportunities in Enterprise Architecture: Insights from 950 + LeanIX Customers

Adina Aldea[✉]

LeanIX, Prins Bernhardplein 200, 1097 JB Amsterdam, The Netherlands
adina.aldea@leanix.net

Abstract. Data-driven architecture is a new paradigm promoted by LeanIX that focuses on making Enterprise Architecture accessible to a wider audience of stakeholders in organizations, to increase data quality and provide transparency when undergoing organizational transformations. This democratization of Enterprise Architecture allows organizations to transform faster and take advantage of trends such as the API Economy, Software-as-a-Service, and Citizen Developers with low-code applications. From this perspective, in this paper, we present the most common challenges that organizations face in their Enterprise Architecture practice due to siloed information and lack of communication between stakeholders. Furthermore, using tools like Excel and PowerPoint to manage the architecture poses challenges due to obsolete data, inability to create meaningful analyses and having multiple sources of truth. In the case of C&A, Helvetia and Marc O'Polo we present how having a modern data-driven Enterprise Architecture has helped these organizations with addressing their challenges and transforming quickly. Finally, we present our ideas on avenues for advancing the field of Enterprise Architecture from a research and practice perspective.

Keywords: Data-driven Enterprise Architecture · Enterprise Architecture challenges · Enterprise Architecture opportunities

1 From Model-Driven Enterprise Architecture for Experts to Data-Driven Enterprise Architecture for All Stakeholders

1.1 The Vision Behind Data-Driven Enterprise Architecture

Enterprise Architecture (EA) is a discipline that aims to help organizations better understand their current IT and process landscape and to provide guidance on how to reach and maintain their desired future state. Traditionally, EA has been a model-driven discipline intended mostly for technical experts who work with modelling languages, such as ArchiMate. However, in the past decade, there has been a paradigm shift from model-driven to data-driven EA, led by tools such as LeanIX.

At the core of the LeanIX philosophy is that EA should extend beyond being solely the domain of technical experts, and instead be accessible and comprehensible for all

C. Griffo et al. (Eds.): EEWC 2022, LNBIP 473, pp. 17–30, 2023.
https://doi.org/10.1007/978-3-031-34175-5_2

members of an organization. We believe that the artifacts produced by EA are not only relevant to the EA team but can also be of immense value to all members of the organization, including subject matter experts. By leveraging their expertise, these stakeholders can contribute to the development of a more comprehensive and holistic EA, which can improve the quality of decisions made and ensure that the organization is well-positioned to address future challenges. Additionally, these stakeholders can also benefit directly from the EA artifacts as they provide valuable insights into the organization's operations, capabilities, and dependencies. For instance, stakeholders such as end-users may offer perspectives on user experience or system usability, which could be vital for shaping EA decisions. Emphasizing the inclusion of non-technical stakeholders as sources of valuable information may ultimately lead to a more comprehensive and effective EA practice.

One of the key collaborators of EA practitioners are the members of the procurement team, particularly when procuring software as a service (SaaS) applications. In our experience, many organizations lack visibility into their SaaS licenses and usage, as it is easy for individuals to purchase SaaS applications with a credit card, without the knowledge or oversight of the IT department. We believe that it is crucial for EA practitioners to be involved in the procurement process, assess license and usage information, and identify opportunities to reduce costs and minimize redundant applications.

Moreover, we have observed a trend among organizations, including more traditional organizations like governmental agencies, to develop their own applications through low-code solutions or by having an in-house software development team. As such, it is becoming increasingly essential for EA practitioners to have a broad understanding of these initiatives, how they fit into the overall architecture of the organization, and their impact. By expanding the scope of EA to encompass adjacent fields, EA practitioners can develop more comprehensive, effective EA practices.

1.2 The Democratization of Enterprise Architecture

Due to the importance of collaboration between EA practitioners and other stakeholders, as also emphasized by Gregor Hohpe [1], effective communication is essential for gathering data from diverse sources and achieving a comprehensive understanding of an organization's operations. Furthermore, we believe that EA practitioners should be able to convey complex technical information in a language that is understandable to non-technical stakeholders. By fostering clear and effective communication between stakeholders, EA practitioners can more effectively align IT systems with broader organizational goals and objectives. To facilitate this democratization of EA, we consider several aspects to be important for organizations.

Simplified Metamodel that can be Easily Adopted. While metamodels provided by frameworks such as ArchiMate and TOGAF are very comprehensive and expressive, a simplified EA metamodel that supports the core aspects of EA[1] leads to easier adoption within organizations. Furthermore, we have noticed this also leads to adoption by a

---

[1] The LeanIX metamodel contains 11 concepts that are aligned with TOGAF and ArchiMate, and cover Strategy and Transformation, Business Architecture, Application Architecture, Technology Architecture: https://docs-eam.leanix.net/docs/meta-model.

more extensive range of stakeholders, as seen in some cases where our customers have thousands of stakeholders utilizing EA information on a monthly basis.

Visualizations that are Easy to Understand by all Stakeholders. To support effective communication about EA, visualizations and analyses that can be understood by diverse audiences are key. For example, automatically generated reports that can be easily customized and produced on demand based on data from a central repository can be used by both EA practitioners and business stakeholders to answer questions, such as "What Applications support the organization's Business Capabilities?" and "How much do these Business Capabilities cost?". However, the level of detail needed by more technical stakeholders, such as solution architects, should not be lost. By providing options for drill-downs and diagrams to show the dependencies of architectural elements, more technical stakeholders can (re-)design certain parts of the EA in more detail.

Data Governance and Enterprise-Wide Collaboration Practices. Collaboration is an essential part of data governance for EA, especially for larger organizations. By fostering collaboration, EA teams can ensure that they have access to the necessary data from all relevant sources to make informed decisions. This leads to a more holistic approach to data governance, where everyone plays a role in maintaining data quality and accuracy.

Integration with Specialized Tools and Open APIs. EA practitioners require data from different sources to ensure that they have a holistic overview of the architecture. Thus, integrating data from different sources is critical to their ability to make informed de-cisions and ultimately contribute to the success of the organization. However, it is not sufficient to have data manually maintained in Excel spreadsheets or similar tools, but rather it is necessary to have real-time integrations that enable EA practitioners to per-form accurate and timely analyses.

2   Current Challenges in the Enterprise Architecture Practice

2.1   Trends Impacting the Enterprise Architecture Practice

One of the main challenges that organizations face in their EA practice is the increased pace of organizational transformations. In the past, organizations planned for long cycles (e.g., a year or more) of transformation with only one significant transformational project in scope. However, current insights gathered from our customers show that many organizations now undergo 10 to 20 significant transformations every year. As a result, EA cannot be viewed as a one-time project, but rather as a continuous process (Fig. 1).

There are several major trends that fuel the transition to a continuous transformation of the EA landscape, namely the API Economy, Software-as-a-Service (SaaS), and the Citizen Developer.

API Economy. It refers to the growing trend of businesses utilizing Application Programming Interfaces (APIs) to connect different systems and enable data exchange between them. This results in increased complexity for organizations in terms of

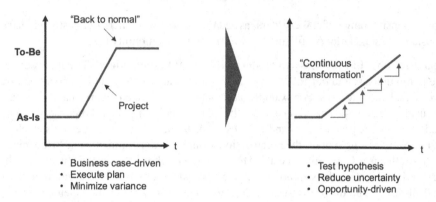

Fig. 1. From long-term single big transformations to continuous transformation of the organizational landscape.

integrating their current application landscape with other applications from their environment.

Software-as-A-Service. The Trend to Transition to the Cloud is One of the Most Influential Factors Affecting the EA Practice. Many Companies View Cloud Solutions as an Easy Way to Modernize Their Landscape and to Eliminate Obsolete Technology that Poses a Lot of Threats. However, Some Industries Have Restrictions that Prevent the Usage of SaaS Applications, Such as the Defense Industry, Due to Regulatory Compliance Factors and Data Security.

Citizen Developer. Another trend that is driving rapid transformation in the EA practice is the increasing adoption of no-code or low-code tools, such as Microsoft Power Apps, Mendix, etc. These tools allow organizations to quickly create applications for specific use cases without needing a full suite of development tools. For instance, a logistics company may create an app that enables warehouse workers to log completed tasks. The data generated from the app can be fed into a central database and analyzed for insights. These types of tools are enabling organizations to rapidly address specific business needs and drive innovation.

2.2 Current Challenges Faced by Organizations

The challenges experienced by companies in implementing an effective EA practice are numerous and varied. Our experience with companies has revealed some common challenges, as follows:

- Many organizations lack a proper EA practice and are relying on information about EA from various stakeholders, represented uniquely using different tools, and stored in multiple repositories. Tools such as Excel spreadsheets, Visio diagrams, and PowerPoint presentations house EA data in different formats, and often those systems are not integrated. This results in siloed information, making it difficult for enterprise architects to easily access EA information required to consistently make informed decisions.

- The process of gathering data for the purpose of producing EA reports is time-consuming, with some organizations taking weeks or months just to do so. These lengthy timeframes make it nearly impossible to produce timely reports on a regular basis (e.g., quarterly). Without EA data that is constantly maintained, the information used to develop reports is often outdated, and worse inaccurate.
- The burden of gathering data often falls on enterprise architects, leaving them with little time to focus on value-adding activities, such as application rationalization, cost-saving initiatives, and innovation.
- Collaboration is also an issue, with enterprise architects often working in isolation and not collaborating effectively with other members of the organization. We have seen instances where enterprise architects have struggled to obtain data from other departments, leading to delays in implementing EA initiatives.
- There is also a lack of alignment between the EA practice and the business, with the latter often making technology-related decisions without consulting the former, especially in the case of purchasing SaaS applications. This can result in unknown risks for the IT department, such as the acquisition of unapproved technology or applications. To cite an example, as part of our work with organizations, we ask them to estimate the number of applications they currently have in their landscape, including SaaS, on-premise, and self-developed applications. Estimating this number can be challenging for many organizations as there is often no centralized repository. This becomes even more difficult for larger organizations that are divided into different entities that operate in silos, resulting in a lack of visibility and transparency that can lead to what is commonly known as Shadow I.T. or Business Managed I.T. This lack of alignment can have significant adverse impacts to an organization, including technology risk, unnecessary costs, and lack of effective tools to support the business operations.

2.3 Maturity Level of the Enterprise Architecture Practice

The maturity level of EA practices varies across organizations. It is noteworthy that many organizations are still quite immature in their approach. In countries like the Netherlands and France, organizations tend to use established EA frameworks such as TOGAF and ArchiMate, as well as reference architectures. However, in other countries, we observe that even large organizations with thousands of employees and hundreds of applications lack an EA practice. Instead, they rely on tools such as Excel, Visio, and PowerPoint, which are not designed for the specific requirements of EA practices. We consider this to the first level of maturity for EA practices, as seen in Fig. 2.

Although many organizations are at the second level of maturity, where they use software tools like LeanIX to manage their EA, integrating data from different systems to create a single source of truth for EA is still a challenge for many. However, for organizations that have a solid foundation for their EA, with data aggregated from different sources, it becomes easier to transform their EA practice to be more business outcome driven and plan the transformation of their landscape accordingly.

While it may seem that having an established EA practice and using software tools for management can indicate the highest level of EA maturity, this is not always the case.

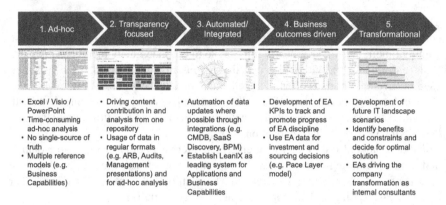

Fig. 2. The maturity levels of the Enterprise Architecture practice.

Without a strong foundation of accessible data, and consistent collaboration with stakeholders throughout the organization, such companies encounter obstacles in transforming their landscape and proving the business value of their EA practice.

3 Success Stories: Solving Enterprise Architecture Challenges with LeanIX

3.1 Defining the Use Cases

When working with an organization to address their EA challenges, it is imperative to first understand their specific problems and needs. To achieve this, we utilize Use Cases that help us relate to their unique issues and provide them with appropriate advice and support. Use cases are often used in the field of EA to better understand the needs and goals of an organization, and to help guide the selection and implementation of technology solutions. They can also be used to communicate these needs and goals to stakeholders within the organization, keeping all parties aligned, and in support of the organization's technology strategy.

One example of a Use Case is Application Portfolio Analysis, which is crucial for organizations starting out in their EA journey. In this case, the focus is on consolidating all applications into a single EA software tool for different types of analysis, such as Functional and Technical Fit, Business Criticality, Cost, Obsolescence Risk, Dependency to other elements in the architecture, etc. Once this is achieved, the next step is Application Rationalization to reduce costs and improve the overall landscape, or to define migration plans to the cloud for greater agility and scalability.

Use Cases are not only useful in understanding problems but also help in suggesting appropriate analysis and visualization techniques that can be shared with different members within the organization. These use cases are also relevant for different stakeholders within the organization, such as enterprise architects, business analysts, solution architects, etc. By understanding these specific needs, we can provide targeted support to help organizations achieve their EA goals.

3.2 IT Modernization at C and A

We conduct regular surveys with our customers to understand the needs and focus areas relating to their EA practice. In a recent survey, we have asked our customers "What should be IT's top priority in 2022?" (Fig. 3). From the 141 responses received, it can be seen that Reducing tech debt / Upgrading their legacy systems is the highest priority. These results are not surprising as many organizations are still using outdated technology and systems. Additionally, the second most common need was migrating to the cloud, which is closely related to legacy system upgrades. Upgrading legacy systems often involves moving to newer cloud-based solutions, which can offer better functionality and scalability compared to on-premise systems. These survey results highlight the importance of modernizing IT systems to keep up with changing technology trends and business needs.

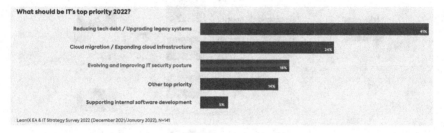

Fig. 3. Results of the survey on top IT priorities for 2022 [2].

C&A is a global retail organization that faced challenges with their IT landscape, which included multiple stores in several countries with complex legacy systems and databases. They used various tools such as Excel, Visio, and PowerPoint for documenting and managing their IT landscape before they realized that it was unsustainable in the long run. Therefore, C&A decided to transition to an omnichannel strategy to compete with other retailers but realized that their current IT landscape was too complex for this strategy.

Their primary goal was to find vendors that provided applications and technologies that were easily configurable for their specific needs in order to replace their legacy landscape. Furthermore, other key requirements included ensuring transparency and accountability in their IT services, avoidance of a siloed organization, help identify redundancies, and reduce costs.

To achieve these goals, they created an EA board, and required the EA team to report to that board. One of their main challenges was collecting the necessary EA data, as it was scattered across different locations with only a subset of essential stakeholders involved. C&A overcame these obstacles by extending the scope of the EA transformation project to the entire organization and ensuring that every employee had access to the information.

With the help of LeanIX, the EA team at C&A managed to easily create monthly reports for the EA board and defined principles for selecting technology vendors and tools, which included criteria related to the impact on the architecture (e.g.: Homegrown or commercial-of-the-shelf software?). Additionally, another important aspect was to analyze the flow of data through the EA landscape. This involved a determination of current integrations as well as development of a plan to extend their integration landscape in the future. C&A recognizes that having this information about their complete integration architecture is essential to determine the complexity of replacing an application in the landscape.

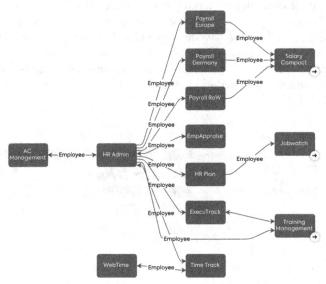

Fig. 4. Data Flow diagram showing how Employee data is exchanged between applications[2].

Figure 4 shows an example of how the flow of data between applications can be visualized and analyzed. Here we see that the HR Admin application is heavily integrated with other applications in the landscape. Therefore, replacing it, while also ensuring no data loss or service disruption, would be a comprehensive and complex task.

This case study highlights the challenges many organizations face when it comes to modernizing their IT landscape. C&A's experience is not unique to the retail sector, and we frequently see similar challenges in other industries. More information about the C&A case is available on the LeanIX website [3].

3.3   Post-Merger Integration at Helvetia

In another one of our customer surveys we have asked organizations how many Merger and Acquisitions (M&A) they perform in a year. The results, which can be seen on the left side of Fig. 5, are quite surprising. Almost 40% of the respondents said that their organizations have at least one M&A and one Carve-out per year. From our experience working with customers, these numbers can be as high as five M&As and/or Carve-outs per year. For these organizations, it is imperative to be very agile in their assimilation of new entities.

---

[2] This is example data and not data from C&A.

M&As require transparency into the organization's landscape to ensure a seamless integration of the acquired company's systems and applications (as seen in Fig. 5). This involves rationalizing the organization's existing applications and identifying any duplicates across the two entities. Moreover, it's essential to establish a clear target landscape for the newly integrated company, outlining the desired state of the organization's technology infrastructure. This process ensures that the M&A activities are carried out smoothly and with minimal disruptions.

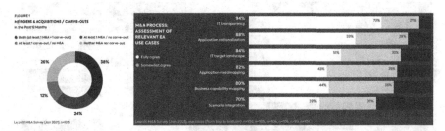

Fig. 5. Number of M&A/Carve-outs per year and aspects that are important for success [4].

Helvetia is a large insurance company based in Switzerland, which merged with Nationale Suise in 2014 to achieve economies of scale and strengthen their position in the market. The management team at Helvetia was keen to explore opportunities within the new landscape and identify areas of synergy. They also needed to assess the current risk profile, especially given the high level of data sensitivity being exchanged throughout the EA landscapes of insurance and banking organizations. Their primary goal was to ensure that their customers did not face any inconvenience during the merger process, and for that, they needed to combine the landscapes of both entities effectively.

However, merging two different landscapes is not an easy task, even if they have the same business processes but use completely different supporting technologies. To tackle this issue, Helvetia used the Atlassian platform, namely Confluence and Jira. They used Confluence to post information about the transformation process within the organization. By embedding LeanIX reports and diagrams, up-to-date information on the transformation was available for the whole organization, which insured the transparency of the process. In addition, they also used Jira to manage tickets regarding the migration process from one application to another. They imported data into LeanIX and created heatmap reports, which provided an overview of the transformation process in relation to different projects, objectives, and the architecture itself.

Before starting this migration, it was essential for Helvetia to analyze all business units from both entities and identify the differences between the applications they used to support the same processes and capabilities. This analysis was critical for the rationalization part of the post-merger integration process, where they would merge the two landscapes. Up-to-date and on-demand analysis and reports were necessary to ensure they had a clear overview of the process.

One of the main reports that Helvetia used was the Application Matrix report, where applications are analyzed in relation to the business capabilities and/or processes they support as well as the business entities that use them. This report allowed them to assess where duplicates from the two entities existed in the landscape, and was the start of their Application Rationalization process.

∨ Customer Relationship				
	After Sales Service	Customer Service	Opportunity, Order & S...	Retention & Loyalty Pro...
Australia	Mailsnake	CustEchoe Europe	salesforce Light	Bonus Card Asia/Pacif...
		issueTrack		Bonus Card Use Watch
Brazil	Mailsnake		salesforce Light	Bonus Card Americas
France		Call Center Managem...	salesforce Light	Bonus Card Europe
		issueTrack		Bonus Card Use Watch
> Headquarter		Call Center Managem...	salesforce Light	
Italy		CustEchoe Europe		Bonus Card Use Watch
Poland		issueTrack		Bonus Card Europe
Spain	Mailsnake	CustEchoe Europe	salesforce Light	
USA	Mailsnake	issueTrack		Bonus Card Americas
				Bonus Card Europe
				Bonus Card Use Watch

Fig. 6. Example of an Application Matrix showing the applications used by the different business units of an organization[3].

Figure 6 shows an example of the applications that support an organization's Customer Relationship capability, and the differences between which applications are used by its business units. For instance, it is noticeable that there is quite a bit of variation in the applications used by different business units for Customer Service. This provides a good baseline for the Application Rationalization process.

Overall, mergers and acquisitions are complex processes that require careful planning, coordination, and execution. With the help of LeanIX, Helvetia was able to streamline their transformation process and ensure that their customers did not face any inconvenience. More information about the Helvetia case is available on the LeanIX website [5].

3.4 SAP S4/HANA Transformation at Marc O'Polo

Another common Use Case for companies is the implementation of big systems like Enterprise Resource Planning (ERP) system. In Europe, many organizations use SAP, while in the United States, Oracle is the most used ERP system. However, regardless of the specific system, many organizations are faced with the challenge of moving from a legacy ERP system to a new one. It's important to note that in many cases, organizations don't have just one ERP system, but rather multiple systems that are not well integrated with each other (see Fig. 7). This lack of integration can create obstacles for the implementation of a new system and highlights the need for proper application portfolio management and integration strategy.

---

[3] This is example data and not data from Helvetia.

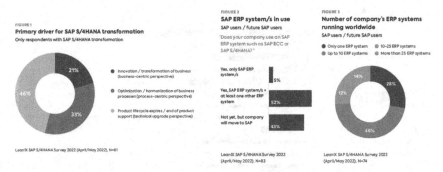

Fig. 7. Number of ERP systems in use and the main driver for the SAP S4/HAHA transformation [6].

Marc O'Polo, a global fashion brand and retailer, faced a different problem compared to C&A. They had been using localized ERP systems, which they realized was not an efficient solution. As a result, they decided to move to SAP S4/HANA, which required them to transform their entire architecture. This is a common problem faced by many companies undergoing ERP transformations.

The old and new systems needed to work in tandem for a long time to ensure that there was no loss of service or data, which could cause the organization to a loss of revenue and reputation due to customers being unhappy with the disruption. The two critical parts of the transformation were maintaining employee involvement and motivation and completing the project within two years. The employee involvement and motivation were crucial because this was an intensive project, and the employees had to be retrained and work with two different systems at the same time.

To stick to the two-year deadline, the company had to be able to quickly import data about their EA in LeanIX and onboard 80 employees. The most important aspect that made this complex transformation a success was the collaboration between the business and IT teams, which was made possible by having transparency of information presented in easy to use and understand reports and diagrams.

One of the reports that help plan such complex transformations is the Project Roadmap, where organizations can see the dependencies between projects and also do a drill down to the affected applications and technologies. Figure 8 shows a Project landscape with transformations related to the implementation of the SAP S4/HANA system and the impact on the current application landscape.

One interesting aspect of this transformation was that Green IT was a priority for Marc O'Polo. They were very conscious of their carbon footprint and considered IT within the scope of their sustainability strategy. Green IT not only helps reduce an organization's carbon footprint, but it also has several other benefits such as reduced energy consumption, cost savings, improved reputation, and compliance with regulations. By integrating green IT principles into their EA, organizations can ensure that their IT systems and infrastructure are designed with sustainability in mind. This can involve using energy-efficient hardware, virtualization, cloud computing, and other technologies that help reduce energy consumption and carbon emissions. As sustainability continues to be

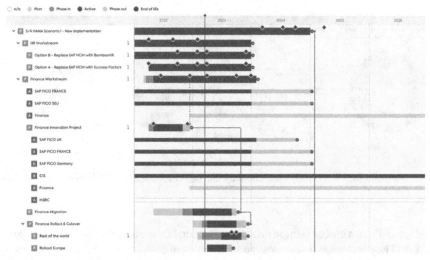

Fig. 8. Project Roadmap with SAP S4/HANA related projects[4].

a critical concern for businesses, incorporating green IT into EA will become increasingly important for organizations to remain competitive and socially responsible. More information about the Marc O'Polo case is available on the LeanIX website [7].

4 Advancing the Field of Enterprise Architecture: Opportunities for Research and Practice

4.1 IT Sustainability as a Key Priority

One emerging topic in the field of EA is sustainability. This is not just an environmental issue, but it is also becoming a business imperative. As a result, there are many opportunities for research and practice in this area.

One of the key findings from a recent survey of 128 respondents is that companies are starting to consider sustainability also from an IT perspective [2]. However, there is still a long way to go. A major issue is that IT is often overlooked when it comes to sustainability. This is partly due to a lack of understanding about what IT can do to help companies become more sustainable.

For example, a survey from Capgemini found that only 40% of companies knew their CO2 footprint [8]. This indicates that many companies are not even aware of the environmental impact of their IT operations. Furthermore, less than 20% of companies had a formal sustainability strategy in place.

In order to achieve sustainability goals within an organization, there are several questions that can be asked to guide the implementation process. For example, "Which capabilities are essential to achieve the sustainability goals within your organization?" and "How do you actually implement these capabilities within your organization from

---

[4] This is example data and not data from Marc O'Polo.

the point of view of your architecture?". From the perspective of the architecture, this may involve looking at the current architecture and identifying areas where it can be optimized. This could involve rationalizing applications to remove duplication and reduce resource consumption, developing a migration strategy to move to more sustainable technologies such as cloud-based solutions, avoiding having SaaS licenses for applications that are only used by a few people, or even improving code efficiency for self-developed software.

Given the importance of this topic, there is a clear need for more research and guidelines for practitioners in the area of sustainability and IT. For LeanIX, as an EA software tool vendor, there is also an opportunity to help companies become more aware of their environmental impact and to provide them with the tools and resources they need to become more sustainable [9]. Ultimately, this will not only benefit the environment, but also the long-term success of businesses.

4.2 Better (Automated) Risk and Security Analyses

The field of risk and security is not a new concept, and many organizations are increasingly interested in supporting security frameworks and improving risk and security analyses, particularly with more automated approaches. In a recent survey we performed, 72% of respondents stated that improving their risk assessment capabilities is a priority for them [2]. While previous attempts have been made in this regard [10], there is still significant room for improvement in these areas, highlighting the need for more advanced and automated risk and security analyses.

4.3 Artificial Intelligence and Machine Learning for Enterprise Architecture

Artificial Intelligence (AI) and Machine Learning (ML) are increasingly shaping the field of EA, as architects are required to transform the EA of their organizations to accommodate internal initiatives involving data science practices. For example, enterprise architects need to ensure that the organization has the necessary infrastructure and systems to handle the volume, variety, and velocity of data generated by data science initiatives. Additionally, they need to ensure that these tools and technologies are integrated with the organization's existing systems and applications to enable seamless data flow and processing.

An interesting avenue to explore is how AI and ML can be used to improve the modeling and analysis of EA models. For example, analyzing the current architecture, identifying modeling patterns and making recommendations for specific improvements, or making suggestions while modeling to adhere to certain modeling principles that the organization is using. Additionally, AI and ML can be used to create documentation for EA models and to interrogate models in a conversational manner by non-experts, similar to how the Generative Pre-trained Transformer models from OpenAI can be used for text [11].

One possible avenue is exploring how these technologies can help improve modeling within EA, including identifying new design patterns and suggesting design solutions for specific situations. This is an area that requires further exploration, and discussions are needed to generate insights and recommendations that can help advance the field of EA.

References

1. Hohpe, G.: The Software Architect Elevator: Redefining the Architect's Role in the Digital Enterprise. O'Reilly Media, Inc. (2020)
2. LeanIX report on From Technical Debt to Sustainability: Enterprise Architects on IT Priorities for 2022, https://www.leanix.net/en/download/enterprise-architects-on-it-priorities-2022, last accessed on 2023/03/27
3. LeanIX website, C&A customer story, https://www.leanix.net/en/customers/success-stories/c-and-a, last accessed on 2023/03/27
4. LeanIX report on The Role of Enterprise Architects in M&A, https://www.leanix.net/en/download/the-role-of-enterprise-architects-in-mergers-acquisitions, last accessed on 2023/03/27
5. LeanIX website, Helvetia customer story, https://www.leanix.net/en/customers/success-stories/helvetia, last accessed on 2023/03/27
6. LeanIX report on SAP S/4HANA Survey 2022, https://www.leanix.net/en/download/sap-s4-hana-report-2022, last accessed on 2023/03/27
7. LeanIX, website, Marc O'Polo customer story, https://www.leanix.net/en/customers/success-stories/marc-o-polo, last accessed on 2023/03/27
8. Capgemeni report on Sustainable IT: https://www.capgemini.com/wp-content/uploads/2021/05/Sustainable-IT_Report.pdf
9. Sundberg, N., Barnekow, H.: Sustainable IT Playbook for Technology Leaders: Design and implement sustainable IT practices and unlock sustainable business opportunities. Packt Publishing Ltd. (2022)
10. Aldea, A., Hacks, S.: Analyzing Enterprise Architecture Models by Means of the Meta Attack Language. In: Advanced Information Systems Engineering: 34th International Conference, CAiSE 2022, Proceedings, pp. 423–439. Springer International Publishing, Leuven, Belgium, June 6–10, 2022
11. OpenAI GPT-4 website, https://openai.com/product/gpt-4, last accessed on 2023/03/27

Presented Papers

A New Action Meta-model and Grammar for a DEMO Based Low-Code Platform Rules Processing Engine

David Aveiro[1,2,3]($\boxtimes$) (iD) and Vítor Freitas[1,3]($\boxtimes$) (iD)

[1] Technology and Innovation, ARDITI - Regional Agency for the Development of Research, 9020-105 Funchal, Portugal
daveiro@uma.pt, vitor.freitas@arditi.pt
[2] NOVA-LINCS, Universidade NOVA de Lisboa, Campus da Caparica, 2829-516 Caparica, Portugal
[3] Faculty of Exact Sciences and Engineering, University of Madeira, Caminho da Penteada, 9020-105 Funchal, Portugal

Abstract. We consider current Design and Engineering Methodology for Organizations (DEMO) Action Rules Specification to be unnecessarily complex and ambiguous. Even while using a "structured English" syntax similar to the one used in Semantics of Business Vocabulary and Business Rules (SBVR), such specifications are: incomplete while not containing enough ontological information to derive a functional implementation; and complex by containing mostly unneeded specifications. We propose a new meta-model for DEMO's Action Model in the form of an Extended Backus–Naur Form (EBNF) syntax which is being implemented in a prototype that directly executes DEMO models as an Information and Workflow System. This prototype includes an action engine that runs DEMO transactions and the enclosed actions specified in our approach. We are currently integrating Blockly in our solution to allow syntactically correct visual programming of our proposed new Action Rule language that includes constructs to evaluate logical conditions, update the state of internal or external information systems, obtain input and provide output (formatted with a 'What You See Is What You Get' (WYSIWYG) template editor) to users, among others.

Keywords: enterprise engineering · DEMO · meta model · action model · action rules

1 Introduction

Numerous studies find that many software projects fall short of end customers' initial expectations. From [1], where certain case studies were conducted, a survey of 800 IT managers [2, 3] revealed that 63% of software development projects failed, 49% went over budget, 47% cost more to maintain than anticipated, and 41% fell short of meeting user and business requirements.

C. Griffo et al. (Eds.): EEWC 2022, LNBIP 473, pp. 33–52, 2023.
https://doi.org/10.1007/978-3-031-34175-5_3

Dalal et al. examined a number of project failure-related reports that have been published and built a list of failure factors that are responsible for this high failure rate [4]. Unrealistic project objectives, incomplete requirements, a lack of stakeholder and user involvement, issues with project management and control, an inadequate budget, changing requirements, inconsistent requirements and specifications, a lack of planning, poor communication, and the use of new technologies for which software developers lacked the necessary experience and expertise are common causes.

An enterprise engineering method called DEMO [5] is linked to a strong body of theories which intend to address the challenges highlighted above. Despite how sound DEMO is in theory, there are still many legitimate concerns regarding its utilization. DEMO's Action Model (AM), which is hardly ever employed in projects, is one of the fundamental components and one of the theoretical foundations that is frequently overlooked in current practice [6]. This occurs despite the fact that the methodology's creator himself regards the AM as the most significant model and where all model information is contained in detail [5, 7]. It is regarded as the organization's differentiator model, or what makes it special. And from this model one can elicit all other three aspect models of DEMO.

In this paper we propose a new Action Meta-Model and Grammar for a DEMO based low-code platform rules processing engine by evolving the DEMO Action Model with the proposal of a new meta-model in the form of a EBNF syntax which is currently being implemented in our DEMO based low-code platform, DISME (Direct Information Systems Modeller and Executer).

We claim that the way Action Rules are currently specified in DEMO, result in incomplete specifications that maintain ambiguity and do not contain enough ontological information for direct generation of information systems, as claimed by DEMO's propounder. With our proposal, we can describe, still on an ontological level, a wider range of crucial details and information, enabling a nearly direct execution of models as an information system. As a result, we help close the enormous gap between DEMO models and the significant implementation issues that surface during the software development process and which should be described right away along with ontological elements. Applying our proposal in a low code platform we are developing, by executing models directly, we drastically shorten the time it takes to produce information systems. And thanks to the use of DEMO as our core conceptual foundation, we have, as a starting point, a more complete elicitation of requirements, one of the main reasons Informations Systems projects fail. We demonstrate and validate our contribution using the EU-rent case [8].

2 Research Method

According to Design Science Research by A. R. Hevner [9, 10], the Information Systems Research paradigm used in this study should be viewed as a collection of three closely related cycles of activities.

On Fig. 1, these activities are depicted. Hevner argues that these three activities should not be used separately because only together do they provide a solid design science research and can produce a reliable result. Our research, with regards to the

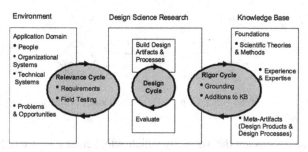

Fig. 1. Design science research cycles [10]

first cycle, Relevance, which is depicted in Fig. 1, revealed a glaring issue of ambiguity and a lack of concise and crucial information regarding the current syntax of DEMO Action Rules. As a result, an opportunity to design a more comprehensive syntax was at hand. We devised a new grammar for DEMO's Action Rules with relation to the second design cycle. This grammar was developed following numerous iterations of exhaustive and thorough design, implementation, and evaluation of various language elements, as well as testing them in the action executer engine in our prototype using both the EU-Rent case and a real-world project being developed in a nearby private company. We propose a new Action Meta Model for DEMO that, in our opinion, will allow the development of Action Rule Specifications in a more thorough and complete manner. Finally, the theoretical underpinnings of DEMO itself provide support for the studies about the final third cycle, Rigor.

3   Background and Theoretical Foundations

DISME uses DEMO methodology as a solid foundation for the production of collaborative-based organizational models and diagrams for the specification of its pro-cesses, information flow, responsibilities of both human and software, proce-dures and other kinds of organizational artifacts [11].

3.1   DEMO'S Operation, Transaction and Distinction Axioms

According to the operation axiom of the Ψ-theory [12], on which DEMO is founded, subjects in organizations execute two different types of acts: production acts that have an impact on the P-world, or production world, and coordination acts that have an impact on the C-world, or coordination world. Subjects are actors performing an actor role responsible for the execution of these acts.These worlds are always in a particular state indicated by the C-facts and P-facts that have transpired up to that point in time.

When active, actors consider the status of the P-world and the C-world. Actors continually strive to fulfill the agenda provided by C-facts. In other words, actors engage in interaction through the creation and management of C-facts. Figure 2 depicts this connection between the actors and the worlds. It illustrates the guiding principle of organizations whose members are dedicated to effectively accomplishing their agenda.

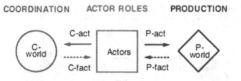

Fig. 2. Interaction of the Actor with the Production and Coordination Worlds [13]

The coordination actions are the means by which actors enter into and uphold commitments towards reaching a given production fact, whereas the production acts contribute to the organization's objectives by bringing about or delivering products and/or services to the organization's environment [14].

The coordinating acts follow a certain path along a generic universal pattern called transaction, in accordance with the transaction axiom of the Ψ-theory [12].

Three phases make up the transaction pattern: (1) the order phase, where the initiating actor role of the transaction expresses his wishes in the form of a request and the executing actor role promises to produce the desired result; (2) the execution phase, where the executing actor role actually produces the desired result; and (3) the result phase, where the executing actor role states the produced result and the initiating actor role accepts that result, effectively closing the transaction.

This succession, which is referred to as the "basic transaction pattern", only takes into account the "happy case", in which everything proceeds as predicted. To realize a new production fact, all five of these steps are essential. The universal transaction pattern that takes into account many more coordination acts, such as revocations and rejections that may occur at any point along the "happy path", is found in [14].

All transactions go through the four social commitment coordination acts of request, promise, state, and accept; however, these steps might be taken tacitly, that is, without any kind of explicit communication taking place. This could occur as a result of the adage "no news is good news" or just plain forgetfulness, both of which can seriously damage a business. Therefore, it's crucial to always take the complete transaction pattern into account while designing organizations. Two distinct actor roles are in charge of transaction steps. The request and accept phases are the responsibility of the initiating actor role, and the promise, execution, and state steps are the responsibility of the executing actor role. The responsible actor may not carry out these steps because the relevant subjects may delegate one or more of the transaction steps that fall under their purview to another subject, even if they are still ultimately liable for such acts [14].

3.2   DEMO Action Rules

DEMO Action Rules are the guidelines for managing events to which actors must react, or business rules. The Action Model of DEMO is not comprised by this set of rules alone, but also contains work instructions regarding the execution of production acts both represented in the Action Rules Specification (ARS) [7]. The Action Rule Specification (ARS) standard has evolved through time, starting with a pseudo-algorithmic language and culminating, in DEMO's specification language 4.5, in a definition which adheres to the Extended Backus-Naur Form (EBNF), the international standard syntactic meta language, defined in ISO/IEC 14977 [15].

The general form to represent an action rule is < event part > < assess part > < response part >. What event (or collection of concurrent events) is reacted to is specified by the event part. An action rule's assess portion is divided into three sections that correspond to the three validity claims: the claims to rightness, sincerity, and truth. The final section, the response, is broken down into an if clause that outlines what must be done if the actor believes that complying with the event is justifiable and, potentially, what must be done if it is not. This method of developing action rules enables the performer to stray from the "rule" if they believe it is acceptable while also being held accountable for it [7].

We consider this way of Action Rules Specification to be ambiguous because, despite using a structured English syntax akin to that found in Semantics of Business Vocabulary and Rules [8], it does so in an imprecise manner that lacks some necessary ontological details to be used as the basis for the implementation of an information system. For instance, as we will discuss in more depth in Sect. 4, it lacks a method to deal with sets of actions or operators. Additionally, the current standard brings unneeded complexity since it includes a lot of extraneous details about three different forms of evaluation: fairness, sincerity, and truth. The following section, in which we go into more detail about our proposal will develop these claims.

4 Direct Information Systems Modeller and Executer

Three main components primarily make up DISME: 1) a Diagram Editor to create the higher level DEMO models in a graphical way 2) the System Manager to precisely detail and parametrize all DEMO Models, with a special attention to the Action Model, so that a complete information system can be specified according to an organization's demands; and 3) The System Executer to directly run the modeled information system in production mode.

In the System Manager, one or more users assume the administrator role and have the ability to modify each organizational process by creating and editing transactions, their relations, action rules and input forms that are associated with these transactions, in specific transactions steps, as well as by specifying entity and property types, that is, the main business objects and their attributes, or, in other words, the database of the information system. Users who model the system just need a basic understanding of enterprise engineering modeling, which is similar to the "language / representation" used within businesses, rather than requiring specific programming skills.

Users who have been granted authorization to participate in transactions in the System Executor do so in accordance with their roles and following DEMO's transaction pattern. The System Executor can be broken down into two main components: 1) the Dashboard, which serves as the user interface for users to interact with when performing organizational tasks, and 2) the Execution Engine, which controls the information and process flow in accordance with the full specification of the system.

The Dashboard interface can be seen in the following figures. In Fig. 3, it is shown where the user can start new processes, depending on the process types existing in the system and the current user's permissions. Here, it is also possible to see a section responsible for counting the pending and performed tasks, as well as delegations made.

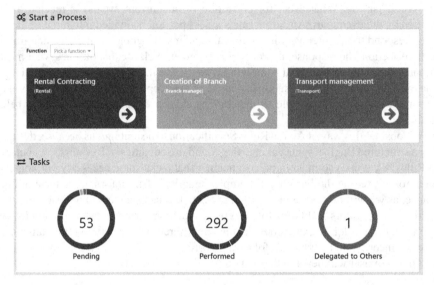

Fig. 3. Dashboard Interface - Start Process and Task Counting

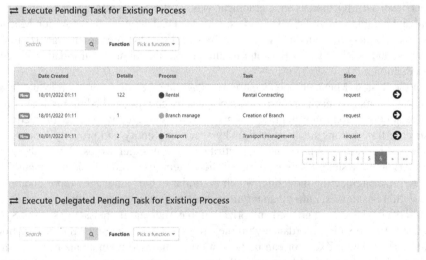

Fig. 4. Dashboard Interface - Pending Tasks

Figure 4 represents the Dashboard sections where users can look at their pending organizational tasks' data, such as creation date, the process it belongs to, the associated transaction type and state. Also, this is where the Execution Engine is incorporated so that the user can execute the tasks shown in the table rows.

The development of the database behind the prototype solution was heavily influenced by the DEMO way of thinking, trying to capture the essence of an organization's workflow, but without abstracting from their infological and datalogical implementations. One of the goals was to keep the platform as flexible as possible in terms of the editing possibilities available [16].

5   New Action Rule Syntax Specification and Implementation

In Table 1, we present, in EBNF[1], the current result of our iterations of development of a syntax and constructs specification of DEMO Action Rules which are runnable, in relation to its previous version [11]. We next introduce how this grammar corresponds to a set of requirements for the respective implementation of the DISME's engine that runs the action rules, and consequently, all the logic used for the implementation of their visual programming. In this specification presented in the table below, new concepts are highlighted in bold and updated ones are in italic.

An action rule occurs in the context of a transaction type, among those specified in the system, in the activation of a particular transaction state. An action rule can lead to the execution of one or more actions of a specific type. For example, an action may imply a causal link - changing the state of any transaction - or it may simply assign a value to a property in the system. We can have a sequence of one or more actions. For each action, one needs to specify the action type that will imply what concrete operations/instructions will be executed by the action engine and then define its parameters, specific to the corresponding action type, required for its execution.

An action can be specified that will prompt the user for input through a form, that is, for the user to *input* some data for a certain process instance. This form will be designed in the form management component of DISME, shown in Fig. 5, according to the *properties* associated with the respective action. It is also possible to specify, for each property in the form, *enabling conditions, validation conditions and form computing*. *Enable conditions* are used when we want that a property is "hidden/disabled" from the form unless the specified condition is true, which in that case the property will be shown. *Validation conditions* have to be satisfied/validated so that the user can submit the form data, being that if the condition is not satisfied, a message is presented back to him. *Form computing* enables us to define computations regarding data in the current form for a specific field, with that property being filled automatically based on the given expression instead of a manual fill by the user.

As opposed to the last action type mentioned, one can also define actions that will *output* information to the user. Using a WYSIWYG editor to create a new template or selecting an already saved template from the system's database, we can output a custom notification or dialog box directly to the user when the action rule is run. The possibility

---

[1] https://en.wikipedia.org/wiki/Extended_Backus%E2%80%93Naur_form

Table 1. Action Model EBNF specification (column separation equals the EBNF symbol " = ")

when	WHEN transaction_type IS|**HAS-BEEN** *transaction_state* { action} -
transaction_type	STRING
transaction_state	REQUESTED | PROMISED | EXECUTED | DECLARED | ACCEPTED | DECLINED | REJECTED | REVOKE_REQUEST_REQUESTED (...[2])
action	*causal_link* | assign_expression | *user_input* | **edit_entity_instance** | *user_output* | produce_doc | if | *API_CALL*
user_output	STRING
produce_doc	static_template | form_template
static_template	STRING
form_template	STRING
assign_expression	property " =" (term | property_value)
property	STRING
causal_link	transaction_type MUST BE transaction_state [min [max]] **[CANCEL_PROC] [CONTINUE_IF_SAME_USER]**
min	Integer
max	Integer | *
user_input	{ form_property}-
edit_entity_instance	{entity_detail} { form_property}-
form_property	property [form_calculation] [enable_condition] {validation_condition} [MANDATORY]
entity_detail	property
form_calculation	compute_expression
enable_condition	ENABLE condition
validation_condition	[NOT] validation_condition_type user_output
validation_condition_type	REQUIRED | IS_NUMBER | IS_INTEGER | EQUAL_TO | MAX_WORD_LENGTH | LESS_EQUAL | HIGHER_EQUAL | HIGHER_THAN | LESS_THAN | MIN_LENGTH | BELONG_SRANGE | MAX_LENGTH | MIN_WORD_LENGTH | HAS_CHARACTER | REG_EXPRESSION | HAS_WORD | IS_EMAIL | IS_URL | CUSTOM_VALIDATION
compute_expression	term {compute_operator term}-

(continued)

---

[2] All other c-facts of the transaction pattern are here, but omitted for space reasons.

Table 1. (*continued*)

when	WHEN transaction_type IS|**HAS-BEEN** *transaction_state* { action} -
compute_operator	" +" | " -" | "*" | "/" | "^"
if	IF condition THEN { action} - [ELSE { action} -]
condition	(ISTRUE | NOT evaluated_expression | condition) | (AND | OR { evaluated_expression | condition}-)
evaluated_expression	comp_evaluated_expression | user_evaluated_expression
comp_evaluated_expression	term logical_operator term | property_value
user_evaluated_expression	STRING
logical_operator	" <" | " >" | " = =" | "! ="
property_value	STRING
term	constant | value | property | query | compute_expression | produce_doc
constant	value_type STRING
value	value_type STRING
value_type	TEXT | INTEGER_NUMBER | REAL_NUMBER | BOOLEAN | ENUM | DATE | TIME
query	STRING { term}
while	WHILE condition { action} -
foreach	FOREACH set { action} -
set	"set of elements"

to add properties to this editor, whose value is filled in the running of the action rule, thus making this a dynamic template, isn't yet implemented but is planned to be included in a future iteration of the DISME.

It is also possible to specify '*if then else*' flows, and in the *condition* one can specify complex conditions containing *logical condition*s evaluated automatically by the executor engine or *informal expressions* evaluated by the human user responsible for the transaction step as true or false, or a combination of both. *While* and *For each* kinds of flows are not yet implemented in the prototype but are also planned to be included in a future iteration.

The terminal symbols presented as string and set of elements are automatically parsed and interpreted by the action engine of DISME. The *set of elements* can be a group/array of elements that can be obtained from a customized query that returns a set of elements from the internal and/or external information system.

An important innovation in the action rules syntax is the realization that one needs to decompose a "normal" action rule into two action rules for each transaction state,

Fig. 5. Form Editor

one regarding the act itself and another for the respective fact created. This duality is achieved with the usage of the *IS* and *HAS-BEEN* terms when defining the root of the action rule, as can be seen in the first row of the EBNF table. We came to this realization while noticing that an actor, while executing a certain c-act or the p-act itself, will need to create some original fact(s) (e.g. input in a form while executing a request); and while dealing with a c-fact/p-fact having been executed, it might be needed to have complex conditions evaluation and also new facts creation or computation. It is also worth noting that the responsible role for the HAS_BEEN action rule is the opposite from the one responsible for the IS action rule while in the same transaction state, that is, if it is the initiating role of the transaction that is responsible for the IS action rule, it will be the executing role that will be responsible for the HAS_BEEN action rule of the same transaction state, and vice-versa. This allows an even more clear separation of responsibilities in DEMO models.

Another relevant addition to this syntax is the inclusion of the new *edit entity instance* action type. By carrying out demonstrations and trials of DISME's usage on information systems in a real scenario, it became apparent that an action for editing previously filled data, more specifically entity instances, was needed, especially in a data intensive, and not so process intensive, information system. With this action, the user can specify Action Rules that comprise the modification of editable properties, that is, properties that have the 'editable' flag active, belonging to entity instances created formerly in the current process instance. Also, properties, or entity details, can be specified to be shown in the entity selection modal's select box that will appear on the execution of this action type, in order to give context and facilitate the selection. The transaction type 'Edit Car Information' is an illustration of this. It allows one to change properties like a car's rental pricing and mileage. When creating a transaction instance of this type, the vehicle being edited has to be chosen from a dropdown list. Here, the entity details are the chosen characteristics that would be listed underneath each option, such as its color, to further specify which Car it belongs to, allowing the user to choose the appropriate option, for instance, if there were two identical cars.

Some flags were also added to the *causal link* action specification that handle how the executor engine should behave when running this type of actions, namely the *'cancel process'* and the *'continue if same user'* flags, that refer to whether the causal_link action cancels the current process, for example on the passage of a transaction to the 'quit' state, and whether the execution engine should take the user directly to the execution of the transaction step specified in the causal link, when it reaches this action, in case the current user in the engine's thread is also responsible for that step. The latter flag could be applied, for example, to the first causal link depicted on Fig. 6. In this scenario, due to this causal link action, if the car was deemed to be damaged, the Execution Engine would automatically execute the action rule related to the task "Damage Handling is Requested" as soon as it was generated, instead of continuing the execution of this action rule with the evaluation of the next 'if' statement's condition. This is very important in terms of usability, since the process can flow naturally between different transactions without the user needing to go back to his main dashboard and search for the new action rule that needs his or her input. In this type of action, *minimum* and *maximum* are optional and by default come pre-filled as 1. They indicate how many transactions should result from the current action, whereas if minimum doesn't exist, by default is equalled to 1 and.if maximum doesn't exist, by default is equalled to minimum.

```
WHEN 'Car drop-off' HAS_BEEN stated
IF ['car is damaged']
THEN
    ASSIGN_EXPRESSION 'car damage' = true
    CAUSAL_LINK 'Damage Handling' [must be] requested
ELSE
    ASSIGN_EXPRESSION 'car damage' = false
IF ['current date' > 'contracted drop-off date']
THEN
    ASSIGN_EXPRESSION 'late return penalty' = true
    ASSIGN_EXPRESSION 'late return penalty charge' = EXPRESSION
ELSE
    ASSIGN_EXPRESSION 'late return penalty' = false
IF ['Actual drop off branch' == 'Contracted drop-off branch]
THEN
    ASSIGN_EXPRESSION 'location penalty' = false
ELSE
    ASSIGN_EXPRESSION 'location penalty' = true
    ASSIGN_EXPRESSION 'location penalty charge' = EXPRESSION
IF ['late return penalty' == true OR 'location penalty' == true]
THEN
    CAUSAL_LINK 'Penalty Payment' [must be] requested
```

Fig. 6. Action rule to handle the transaction step 'Car drop-off has been stated'.

An example of an action rule definition, adapted to the last iteration of our Action Rule's Syntax, can be seen in Fig. 6.

After the first 'if' statement, an informal expression that needs to be evaluated by a human user physically inspecting the car and comparing it to the damage sheet signed at pickup can be found. In the event that there is freshly observed damage on the vehicle, a boolean property in the rental instance gets the value true written to it before a transaction to handle the issue is requested. This property serves as a flag in the rental entity and can then later be used to make general queries about rentals with or without damage. We then have a couple 'if' actions that automatically evaluate whether penalties should be applied. In case penalties are to be applied, mathematical expressions can be specified to calculate them automatically, by the engine, that take into consideration properties from the current process. In determining whether there is a location penalty, one can see the usefulness of having our "dual" specification of action rules for each transaction stat. In this case we can be sure to have the organizational facts that originated from the 'Car drop-off IS stated' transaction step which are then needed in this HAS-BEEN action rule. More specifically the 'Actual drop off branch' property would be a fact produced in the IS action rule and not in the HAS-BEEN rule. This need of having actions and facts in both "parts" of a transaction state was "disguised" with the term "WITH" in the current and limited ARS of DEMO. To conclude this action rule, we have another 'if' statement that starts a transaction to handle the penalty payment if needed.

6   DISME'S Components

Three components were implemented in DISME to enable the implementation of our new action rule format: 1) Action Rules Management, 2) Templates management, 3) Forms Management. Then, an Execution Engine was developed to automatically run action rules defined in the former components and a Dashboard was created that integrates its functionality and provides the interface with which users interact in organizational tasks. Due to space limitations, focus will be given in this paper to the Action Rules Management Component and to the Execution Engine.

6.1   Action Rules Management Component

In order to define a component that allowed the visual programming of these Action Rules, the Blockly library was used. Blockly is a library that adds a visual code editor to web and mobile applications. The Blockly editor uses interlocking, graphical blocks to represent code concepts like variables, logical expressions, loops, and more. It allows users to apply programming principles without having to worry about syntax or the intimidation of a blinking cursor on the command line [17]. It thus allows, as is the goal of this component in DISME, managers or individuals in a comparable position in organizations to develop Action Rules that are then saved and used in the execution engine through the Dashboard component, even if they have little or no prior programming experience. The choice of this library was also due to the fact that it is compatible with all the main browsers, i.e. Chrome, Firefox, Safari, Opera, and IE and that it is highly customizable and extensible [18].

This component is responsible for the creation, editing and consequent storage of action rules for a transaction type in a specific transaction state. Another important feature available on this component is one that allows us to see all previously created action rules and, if needed, load them onto the visual programming editor for editing.

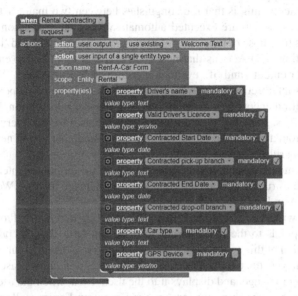

Fig. 7. Design of an action rule using the visual programming component.

An example of the definition of an action rule using this component can be seen in Fig. 7. This example represents the first transaction on a Rental process, that is, the presentation of a welcoming text to the user and then the filling of a form containing the main information from the rental and the renter.

6.2   Execution Engine

The Execution Engine has the function of executing action rules previously defined in the action rules management component through visual programming. This component had already been developed in a previous iteration of the DISME prototype, under the name of 'Expression Engine', due to the fact that its development was more focused on the evaluation of formal expressions. However, it was decided to restructure it due to the expansion of the requirements, previously expressed in EBNF syntax, and, consequently, of the system's database, which significantly affected this component and made its operationalization easier and more efficient.

The Execution Engine is called when a user wants to execute an organizational task, i.e. a set of actions of a transaction in a specific transaction state, through the Dashboard component that provides the interface with which users interact for executing organizational tasks which they are responsible for. When called, the Execution Engine checks if this is a task whose execution is currently starting, in which case it fetches the first action of the action rule associated to it, or if it is a task whose execution has already started, in which case it fetches the action that was pending in the last execution or the action next to the last one performed, according to the action log that is generated by the DISME. Subsequently, it analyzes the type of action to be evaluated, and executes operations accordingly.

Also worth mentioning is that it distinguishes between two major action types: 1) Automatic Actions, which are executed automatically by the Execution Engine, and comprise actions like those of type 'assign expression', 'causal link' and 'if - evaluation of logical conditions'; 2) Actions that necessarily require humN intervention, namely 'user input', 'user output', and 'if - evaluation of informal expressions'. When the Execution Engine is interpreting an action rule, it will execute the corresponding actions automatically until it encounters an action that requires user intervention. When it finds one of these actions, execution flow is returned to the user for its intervention. After doing so, the automatic execution resumes until it finds another action needing human input or the action rule comes to its end.

We'll now demonstrate and give an example of how the dashboard interface uses the execution engine to run an action rule definition and manage its flow. We'll apply the action rule shown on Fig. 7 for this example.

When a user wishes to execute this 'Rental Contracting IS requested' organizational task, that corresponds to the first transaction to be run on a 'Rental' process, it will fetch the first action of this action rule. This corresponds to a 'user output' action, so the Execution Engine gets the template associated with the action, in this case a dialog box with a welcoming message, and displays it to the user. Then, when the user presses the dialog box's button, completing this action, the Execution Engine will proceed to the execution of the next action of the action rule, which in this case is of the 'user input' type, that is, the presentation of a form to the user for filling in the properties (purple blocks) specified in Fig. 7. The structure of the form to be presented to the user is previously defined in the respective forms management component, after the specification of the action rule. An example of the result of the execution of an action of this type can be seen in Fig. 8 below.

When a user successfully submits the form, the execution engine detects that this is the final action listed in the action rule for that organizational task, marks it as finished, and, following DEMO's standard flow of a transaction, automatically follows a default causal link which starts a new task corresponding to the next transaction state - "HAS-BEEN requested". In case this new task requires human intervention, it will appear in the Dashboard of the users with the organizational role authorized to execute it. If not, the engine proceeds with the automatic execution of the action rules, following the DEMO flow, until it encounters an action that requires human intervention or the transaction comes to an end.

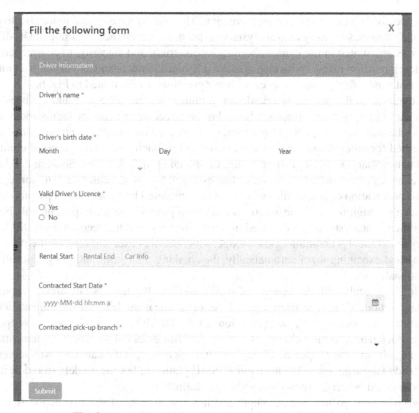

Fig. 8. Execution of a 'user input' action in the Dashboard.

7 Discussion

The specification of Action Rules is created according to the following structure in the current official standard: < event part > < assess part > < response part >. Although it is mentioned [7] that action rules established with the grammar of "structured English" are incredibly simple, it is also stated that some board members appeared perplexed when an action rule with this grammar was presented to them.

One of the grammar's issues lies at the core of its specification. The formulation of these action rules appears to be excessively formal and challenging to comprehend for persons outside the scope of DEMO theory, as well as for new and inexperienced DEMO users.

Comparing it to our approach, we may define a series of actions for an action rule, each with a particular type that indicates what the system should execute/perform in a simpler, literal, structured, and systematic manner, focused on implementation. We contend that the concepts of claims to rightness, sincerity, and truth mentioned in the < assess part > add unneeded ambiguity and complication. With our solution, one can specify a group of structured actions inside an action rule that have an immediate impact on the information system being developed by controlling the necessary process flows, and respective state changes and facts creation. This makes it easier and more effective for collaborators, such as system analysts, who are not aware of the social side of DEMO theory as articulated in the claims about rightness, truth, and sincerity, to comprehend and develop action rules. These claims make it harder to understand and develop action rules that can be fairly complex even with our grammar, as illustrated in Fig. 6.

Compared to the present standard, our grammar is more adaptable and includes a wider range of options and functionalities. For instance, we can specify inputs and outputs to the user, such as prompting a form or displaying information, common actions performed for an organizational process's successful functioning. Our proposal eliminates unnecessary details and complexities of official DEMO ARS, on the other hand it adds complex details which are nevertheless essential for implementation, but thorough visual specification of action rules which can be considered low-code. When pairing our language's straightforward constructions and visual programming component, collaborators such as analysts can specify/design action flows without the need for deep DEMO theory or technical programming knowledge, with DISME's execution engine then interpreting and executing them automatically, thus making their information system fully operational.

Ontology deals with the essence of reality and DEMO theories talk about 'implementation models' derived from higher level ontological models, but implementation models are also ontological. Our extensions of the DEMO meta-model with concepts such as documents, forms, value types, etc. are detailing essential aspects of implementation, but still agnostic of specific IT implementations (say, specific database, web server, client-side language, etc.). We have our DISME platform, but the models stored in its database could be perfectly run by another platform.

We will now go into greater depth about a few aspects of the two action rules' grammar. An action rule presented in the 'structured English grammar' format may be seen in Fig. 9. The < assess part > does not specify causal relationships in its numerous criteria. Due to the fact that we assess and check properties that correspond to a certain entity type connected to the current action being conducted in a straightforward manner, this does not occur in our grammar.

Regarding the < truth > claim, there is no way to specify the outcomes that may happen if each of the conditions is not met. Various actions may be executed in response to various circumstances, and various values may need to be updated, as seen in our example in Fig. 6. Figure 9 and Fig. 6 can be compared, and it is clear that syntax and simplicity are not the strong points of the current DEMO Action Rules' grammar. Additionally, nowhere in the action rule is it stated what consequences may occur if the "Actual drop-off branch" differs from the "Contracted pick-up branch". This action rule, defined in our grammar, as is described in Fig. 6, does not result in this uncertainty, as depending on whether certain conditions are true or untrue, we can describe multiple outcomes. In our case, we can call two different transactions in a way that is not allowed using current DEMO's syntax. Different action types can be specified in our grammar for an action rules' actions, but in this particular case, they are of type 'assign expression', as shown in Fig. 6. In this scenario, if we end up inside the ELSE block, the rental's "location penalty" property will automatically have its value set to "true" whereas the "location penalty charge" property will get its value from a mathematical expression,

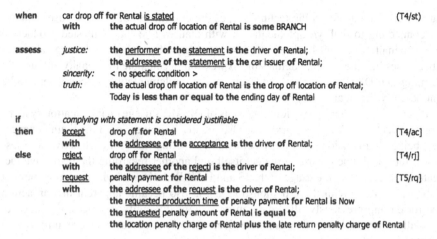

Fig. 9. EU-Rent Action Rule TEOO [7]

which can be an operation between several values, two or more different properties, or a mix of the two.

In the < truth part > displayed in Fig. 9, when an action rule calls for other trans-actions it is not immediately clear which specific condition initiates the call to those transactions or how to manage information, inputs, and outputs. How to perform some-thing of this sort in the TEOO [7] grammar is not at all clear. Many elements of the action rule are redundant or ambiguous, particularly those that begin with the 'with' clause or the rightness claim lines. The addressees and requested production time of a transaction, for example, should not need to be specified as they are already included in the context of the process instance that is carrying out these actions. These add unneeded complex-ity to the action rule. Figure 6 illustrates how our grammar makes it much simpler to understand what conditions and actions call for other transactions, such as the causal link "Penalty payment [must be] requested".

We also find that the use of the 'some' clause under the present standard brings ambiguity. In the case being examined, the context/instance should explicitly define the 'drop-off branch' at run time, negating the need for a distinct specification. DEMO models are purportedly designed to be independent of implementation and/or infologi-cal/datalogical considerations. In previous works we have been defending that DEMO models allow us to abstract from reality and reduce complexity, but they cannot be detached from reality/implementation, and action rules are the ideal place to recognize this relationship.

The DEMO Construction Model is quite detached from implementation since it provides a higher level and comprehensive view of a process as a tree of transac-tions and actor roles. But when it comes to business rules and execution, which are covered in DEMO's Action Rules, a more methodical and simple connection to real-ity/implementation is desperately needed. It is only natural that we "walk the last mile" and allow the specification of implementation details in action rules specification to the point of client output, database updates, and external calls to other systems, in a way that is independent of specific technology, as the current use of 'with' clauses is actually connecting to reality/implementation with clauses like 'the requested production time of penalty payment is Now' and also dealing with infological/datalogical issues with clauses like the one that defines the expression to calculate the penalty amount. So affirming that DEMO models should not include implementation aspects seems to be contradictory/illogical.

By carrying out demonstrations and trials of DISME's usage on information systems in real projects scenarios, our grammar also greatly improved, with the main enhancement being the inclusion of a dual specification of action rules for each activated transaction state, with one regarding the act itself and another regarding the respective fact created, achieved with the usage of the IS and HAS-BEEN terms when defining the root of the action rule. With these demonstrations, it also became apparent that an action type for editing previously filled data, more specifically entity instances, was needed, especially when dealing with a data intensive, and not so process intensive, information system.

According to the GSDP mindset connected with DEMO theories [5], we are actually enabling a highly deep specification of the implementation model that, in a live system, like our DISME prototype, can be run immediately (without any compilation stages).

8   Conclusions and Future Work

As was mentioned above, the Action Rule Syntax we suggest in this paper is more thorough, flexible, and simpler to read, comprehend, implement, and run.

The Action Model is the ideal link between the implementation model and the higher level models (Construction Model and State Model), and is our DISME's main focus. Our approach is superior because it explicitly states what actions will be executed, what inputs or outputs the system will produce, and what asynchronous calls to other transactions or information systems must be made.

The practical engineering approach we are using allows that, with minimal training on language constructs, specialized business analysts are able to scheme their organization's flow in a way that effectively connects strategic high level models with low level details of implementation. These business analysts can then design action rules while also dealing with implementation issues like form design, user output, expression evaluation, and the information system's flow control.

Our current prototype has some outstanding issues, such as allowing the implementation of for/while flows, while making sure that infinite cycles are not met and the incorporation of dynamic elements in templates. We also anticipate that the size and complexity of our grammar will continue to evolve and grow as it has been since its beginning. However, the philosophy that we adhere to and that was discussed in this paper continues to appear to be a promising approach.

In the conference, the presentation of this paper generated lively questions and discussion regarding the needs of improvement in DEMO's Action Meta-model. Most of them were a replication of points raised by the reviewers and our clarifications generated consensus. We adapted the contents of the paper and the replies to the reviewers, taking into account the discussions. One very interesting point raised for discussion was the imperative vs. declarative nature of the Action Rules and the different alternatives of specifying complex branches of actions according to the evaluation of different inter-connected (or not) logical conditions. It was presented to the authors the notion that it is possible to specify different action rules for the same C-fact to comply with different conditions, in order to avoid complex if-then-else trees. However, having important busi-ness logic dispersed in more than one action rule, seems, in our view, to bring unneeded complexity and possible combinatorial explosion [19] in case of need of changes.

Acknowledgments. This work was supported by the Regional Development European Fund (INTERREG MAC), project Dynamic eGov MAC2/5.11a/359.

References

1. Dalal, S., Chhillar, D.R.S.: Case studies of most common and severe types of software system failure. Int. J. Adv. Res. Comput. Sci. Softw. Eng. **7** (2012)
2. Shull, F., et al.: What we have learned about fighting defects. In: Proceedings Eighth IEEE Symposium on Software Metrics, pp. 249–258 (2002). https://doi.org/10.1109/METRIC. 2002.1011343
3. Zeller, A., Hildebrandt, R.: Simplifying and isolating failure-inducing input. IEEE Trans. Softw. Eng. **28**, 183–200 (2002). https://doi.org/10.1109/32.988498
4. Ibraigheeth, M., Fadzli, S.A.: Core Factors for Software Projects Success. JOIV Int. J. Inform. Vis. **3**, 69–74 (2019). https://doi.org/10.30630/joiv.3.1.217
5. Dietz, J., Mulder, H.: Enterprise Ontology: A Human-Centric Approach to Understanding the Essence of Organisation. (2020). https://doi.org/10.1007/978-3-030-38854-6
6. Dumay, M., Dietz, J., Mulder, H.: Evaluation of DEMO and the Language/Action Perspective after 10 years of experience, 29 (2005)
7. Perinforma, A.P.C.: The Essence of Organisation An Introduction to Enterprise Engineering. Sapio Enterprise Engineering. - References - Scientific Research Publishing, Presented at the (2015)
8. Bollen, P.: SBVR: A Fact-Oriented OMG Standard. In: Meersman, R., Tari, Z., Herrero, P. (eds.) OTM 2008. LNCS, vol. 5333, pp. 718–727. Springer, Heidelberg (2008). https://doi. org/10.1007/978-3-540-88875-8_96
9. Hevner, A., R, A., March, S., T, S., Park, Park, J., Ram, Sudha: Design science in information systems Research. Manag. Inf. Syst. Q. **28**, 75 (2004)
10. Hevner, A.: A three cycle view of design science research. Scand. J. Inf. Syst. **19**, (2007)
11. Andrade, M., Aveiro, D., Pinto, D.: Bridging Ontology and Implementation with a New DEMO Action Meta-model and Engine. In: Aveiro, D., Guizzardi, G., Borbinha, J. (eds.) EEWC 2019. LNBIP, vol. 374, pp. 66–82. Springer, Cham (2020). https://doi.org/10.1007/ 978-3-030-37933-9_5
12. Dietz, J.L.G., Mulder, H.B.F.: The PSI Theory: Understanding the Operation of Organi-sations. In: Dietz, J.L.G. and Mulder, H.B.F. (eds.) Enterprise Ontology: A Human-Centric Approach to Understanding the Essence of Organisation, pp. 119–157. Springer International Publishing, Cham (2020). https://doi.org/10.1007/978-3-030-38854-6_8
13. Dietz, J.: Enterprise Ontology: Theory and Methodology. Springer, Berlin Heidelberg (2006)
14. Dietz, J.L.G.: On the Nature of Business Rules. In: Dietz, J.L.G., Albani, A., Barjis, J. (eds.) CIAO!/EOMAS -2008. LNBIP, vol. 10, pp. 1–15. Springer, Heidelberg (2008). https://doi. org/10.1007/978-3-540-68644-6_1

15. 14:00–17:00: ISO/IEC 14977:1996, https://www.iso.org/cms/render/live/en/sites/isoorg/con tents/data/standard/02/61/26153.html, Last Accessed 2 Oct 2022

16. Andrade, M., Aveiro, D., Pinto, D.: DEMO based Dynamic Information System Modeller and Executer: In: Proceedings of the 10th International Joint Conference on Knowledge Discovery, Knowledge Engineering and Knowledge Management. pp. 383–390. SCITEPRESS - Science and Technology Publications, Seville, Spain (2018). https://doi.org/10.5220/000723000383 0390

17. Introduction to Blockly | Google Developers, https://developers.google.com/blockly/guides/ overview?hl=pt, Last Accessed 1 Jan 2022

18. Blockly | Google Developers, https://developers.google.com/blockly, last accessed 2022/10/01

19. Brocade Desktop: irua, https://repository.uantwerpen.be/desktop/irua, Last Accessed 19 Dec 2022

Towards a DEMO Description in Simplified Notation Script

Mark A. T. Mulder$^{(\boxtimes)}$ ⓘ, Rick Mulder ⓘ, and Fiodor Bodnar ⓘ

TEEC2, Hoevelaken, The Netherlands
markmulder@teec2.nl

Abstract. The core methodology of Enterprise Engineering (EE) is Design and Engineering Methodology for Organisations (DEMO) and has been the subject of modelling tools. This methodology can be split into a method or process part and a notation part, describing the meta-model and its visualisation. The way the notation of the methodology has been described for these tools has been of different detail levels. This paper describes the DEMO notation using the grammar of the Simplified platform as an exercise towards a complete notation grammar that can describe all existing and possibly future notations and also to complete the DEMO notation specification. The grammar is part of the Simplified platform, and the notation is the published definition of the notation part of the DEMO methodology. We have chosen a practical approach to developing the notation script and thinking out-of-the-box by not creating a theoretical box a priori.

Keywords: enterprise engineering · DEMO · modelling tools

1 Introduction

The DEMO [1] method is a core method (based on a theoretically founded method*ology*) within the discipline of EE [2]. The DEMO method focuses on the creation of so-called *essential* models of organisations. The latter models capture the organisational essence of an organisation primarily in terms of the actor roles involved, as well as the business transactions [9] (and ultimately in terms of speech acts [5]) between these actor roles. More specifically, an essential model comprises the integrated whole of four aspect models: the Construction Model (CM), the Action Model (AM), the Process Model (PM) and the Fact Model (FM). Each of these models is expressed in one or more diagrams and one or more cross-model tables. DEMO has strong methodological, and theoretical, roots [1,2,9].

After we built the Plena tool for modelling DEMO in the PhD project of Mulder [7], we continued our research to expand the modelling capability. This research found that the modelling capability could not be expanded within the existing Sparx Enterprise Architect (SEA) tool. We found many problems that

C. Griffo et al. (Eds.): EEWC 2022, LNBIP 473, pp. 53–70, 2023.
https://doi.org/10.1007/978-3-031-34175-5_4

we could not solve within this environment, e.g. functionality support, visualisation support, collaborative work support.

The problem we address in this paper is the complexity of the notations and the
visualisation of that notation that we want to use. The example that we describe
in this paper is about DEMO. DEMO is a method with complex diagrams that
are linked together by the main elements, transactions. The transaction has multiple visualisations, dependent on the context. This makes the visualisation of the
element non-trivial and demands variables for the visualisation. Furthermore, the
description of the diagrams in the DEMO Specification Language (DEMOSL) has
more requirements than the SEA tool can handle, e.g. the transactor and transaction kind that reference the same model element, attributes that are always a part
of an entity and cannot be represented separately like ORM representation, and
multiple visualisations of the same element in the same diagram. Other notations
have similar issues (e.g. BPMN swim-lanes and visual attributes, IDEF0 layout
restrictions, ArchiMate double representations). We needed a modelling environment to address all these visualisation issues.

Therefore, we have introduced Simplified modelling platform [6] that can
create models according to specified notations (metamodels) in a web-based
environment and present the models to relevant stakeholders. In summary, the
Simplified modelling platform can contain any model that can be described
as element-connection model with attributes (e.g. data models, process models (blocks and arrows), architecture models). The models can be visualised in
table or diagram style where the representation is free to choose. Although this
paper describes the notationscript from a DEMO method perspective, we have
made notationscripts for more notations (e.g. ArchiMate, BPMN, Flowchart).

In this paper, we report on a study about the configuration effort within the
Simplified modelling platform to support the use of DEMO 3 and 4 in practice
answering the question on the minimal expressive power needed to describe these
notations on this platform. This description should satisfy the model expression
and the visualisation of the models. The flexibility in defining notations can help
to easily define new domain specific notations with new semantics for specific
problems.

Configuring the Simplified modelling platform support for DEMO requires an
elaborate formalisation of the DEMO metamodel, as described in DEMOSL [4],
and further specified to enable the automatic verification of models [7]. In order
to translate the formalised DEMO metamodels, rules and visual notations to the
notationscript we need the notation grammar that will support the definition of
all required concepts and all the related visualisations.

Note that we have described the notation of the methodology in this paper
while not describing any model. The visual and textual representations are part
of the notation description and are represented in the metamodel structure. Also,
we have chosen for a practical approach, thus not studying literature a priori.
This approach might result in a grammar that partially exists. In hindsight, if we
were able to use an available part of an existing notation grammar, then we would
have to combine different parts from these notation grammars, which makes

this option less feasible from a maintenance point of view. Also, the different points of view from different attempts make it very challenging to combine these efforts. Summarising, we have chosen to use our own notation grammar to define notations that will support the definition of required concepts and their related visualisations as will be explained in Sect. 3 and Sect. 6, respectively.

For the visualisation part of the grammar we have looked at implementations of SEA, ADOXX and draw.io. We used the convenient user interface concepts of these implementations and made our own implementation without copying anything.

Because DEMO version 3 and version 4 differ in the number of concepts, metamodel and visualisations we have decided to cover both versions. We see the new concepts of DEMO 4 as an extension on the concepts of DEMO 3 although the literature [3] leaves out options of the previous version [8], e.g. the Organisation Construction Diagram (OCD).

The remainder of this paper is structured as follows. Section 2 describes the research method utilised. Section 3 provides a overview of concepts that are currently supported by the proposed grammar for describing notations. In Sect. 4, we show how how DEMOSL of DEMO version 3.7 has been defined in the notationscript for the CM, PM and the FM. Section 5 addresses the definition of DEMOSL to the notationscript based on DEMO version 4.7.1. In Sect. 6 we continue on the specifics for defining visualisations in a notationscript. Lastly, before concluding, in Sect. 8 we discuss several challenges that future research will have to address.

2   Research Question and Method

The research question was to find a notation to flexibly describe at run-time the meta model of a model notation with the corresponding visualisations. The creation of this notationscript is an iterative process to find a suitable grammar that covers all meta model descriptions. This paper describes the creation of this notationscript which can be seen as an artefact in the sense of design science. We used Design Science Research (DSR) [10] to create the notation grammar and script. This artefact is an object that solves a problem by interaction with the context of that artefact. Thereafter the artefact must be implemented, validated, and evaluated.

3   Notations

Within the Simplified context, a notation can be self-contained, extending or replacing concepts from other notations. By extending other notations, one can add own elements without redefining previous notations. With the replacement functionality, one can restrict the use of a notation to a smaller subset of attributes of the concepts.

We have defined the notation as the highest user meta-level in the Simplified platform. At this level, we can define how models can be modelled and what rules the models must adhere to. In order to verbalise this metamodel, we have created a notation script language and corresponding grammar that can be used to specify notations. The notation script language is described in a notation grammar where the levels of abstraction are reflecting the functional components in the platform, and the transformation between the levels is either interpretation on run-time or compilation when parsing the notation script.

The current version of the notation script has a grammar for the following list of notation concepts which will be explained using the DEMO notations in Sects. 4 to 6.

```
element [extends <refname>] [replaces <refname>]
[comment "<comment>"]
( <name>
<typeRefName> | TEXT | URL | GUID | BOOL | INT | DATETIME
[<default>] [comment "<comment"] [,...] )
```

Listing 3.1. Element Grammar

Element is the base concept often referred to as 'block' (from 'blocks and arrows' in process modelling). In the notation script, the element concept supports the hereafter mentioned parameters. The *elementName* is the display name of the element. The *elementReferenceName* is the unique identifier within the notation. It can *extend* another element, taking the parameters of the extended element in addition to its own. It is also possible to *replace* an element to remove parameters that you do not want to use in your own notation. As in all descriptive concepts there is an option of adding comments. Lastly, an element can have any number of attributes defined, which we will explain later.

Connection is the base concept often referred to as 'arrow' (from 'blocks and arrows'). A connection has two extra parameters on top of the element parameters. The first parameter is *sourceElementReferenceName*, which defines the element of the source element, where the parameter matches the *elementReferenceName* of the referenced element. The second parameter is *targetElementReferenceName*, which defines the element of the target element just like the first parameter.

Typedef is the concept to represent a data type of an attribute (that in turn can be connected to an element or connection). The default supported types are *text, enumeration, boolean, date time, integer, URL,* and *UUID*. Within these types, restrictions on the types and the definition of the values of the enumeration can be added.

Toolbox focuses on the available elements and connections for a specific perspective. Similarly to element, Toolbox has *toolboxName, toolboxReferenceName,* and comments. The *toolboxContentNames* parameter allows the user to define which element and connections should appear. In addition, the *folder* parameter is used to create a categorisation in the toolbox.

```
virtualElement: VirtualKeyword ElementKeyword elementName
    elementReferenceName
  ElementKeyword elementReferenceName
  (ConnectionKeyword connectionReferenceName
   ElementKeyword elementReferenceName)+
  comment?
  ;
```

Listing 3.2. Virtual Element

Virtual Element is the concept of an element that starts to exist when a specific combination of elements and connections starts to exist and are connected. It has the *name* and *referenceName* parameters. In order to define which element and connection compose the virtual element, it has an *elementReferenceName* parameter, followed by one or more *connectionReferenceName* and *elementReferenceName* pairs. It contains the comments parameter like the previous concepts.

Rule is a way to check the restrictions of the model. By defining a logic query on the model, one can generate messages showing rules that have been violated. A rule is defined with a name, and an expression. This expression is a equivalent of a first-order logic expression. It also contains two optional parameters, namely a message can be added in case of rule violation, and comments.

Table is a visualisation of model information in a textual column-shaped format. Tables can be defined to list information in the scope of a repository, model, or a single diagram. Tables have name and Reference parameters. Their content is determined by a selectExpression parameters, which is like first-order logic, similar to rules. The display is handled by tableColumn definitions, which describe the name, span, and reference of the column.

Visual defines the shape of a model element or a model connection that can be displayed on a diagram. The parameters name and ReferenceName are present here. Additionally it has a parameter where a list of diagrams this element can appear on can be specified. The main focus of the visual definition is the visualisationScript, which is further explained in Sect. 6. Optionally there can be comments added.

Diagram is a special element that can hold other elements to visualise a specific perspective of the model. Diagram contains the name and ReferenceName parameters. It has a parameter for elementNames, which specifies the element that are meant to be on the diagram. This enables us to enforce a methodology, or let the user know when they have extra non-standard elements.

Cube is the multi-dimensional textual representation of a part of a model. Currently, a two-dimensional cube, matrix, is the only supported representation.

Behaviour defines the actions in the UI needed to realise the modelling process described in the methodology accompanying the notation. Behaviour is defined by specifying an action, such as adding an element to a diagram, or double clicking something, and a reaction, something that needs to happen in response to the action. It has contains the name parameter, and the behaviour rules parameter. The behaviour rules parameter is build up with an action and reference name, and a reaction and reference name. Optionally there is a final action such as alignment

Attributes can be added to elements, connections, folders, diagrams and virtual elements. The first parameter is the attributeName, which defines the attribute name. This is followed by the attributeType which can be a base type such as defined in typedef at the beginning of this list. In addition, it has the following three optional parameters. AttributeRequired, which defines if this is a mandatory attribute to fill, attributeDefault, which specifies the default value of the attribute, and comments.

Together, we expect these concepts to cover all of DEMO notation visualisations. When we are specifying DEMO 3 and 4 we will report on the current level of success on the specification.

4   DEMO 3 Notation

The notation of DEMO version 3.7 is formalised in DEMOSL [4] and some improvements were proposed in a PhD [7]. The formalisation of the DEMOSL enabled the automated verification and exchange of DEMO models and it has been implemented in the SEA add-on Plena. Whether the discussion on the relevance or usefulness of these concepts of DEMO is a discussion that can be done in another paper. We will focus on using the concepts and visualisation of these concepts as described in the above mentioned literature. The notation script of Simplified for DEMO 3 currently seems to contain all concepts of the aspect models CM, PM, and FM and we will explain the translation from DEMOSL to the notation script in this section. The DEMO 3 notation, as shown in listing 4.1, has been given the version number 3.7. This corresponds to the version of DEMOSL but does include the work of the mentioned PhD.

```
ScriptVersion01
Notation for DEMO version 3.7
comment "This version of DEMO is described in EO, TEOO and DEMOSL 3.7"
```

Listing 4.1. Script

Within DEMO 3, three enumerated data types exist as shown in listing 4.2. These data types describe all states of some attributes of the transaction kind, attribute type, and step kind.

```
typedef TRANSACTIONSORT ENUM (None, Original, Informational,
    Documental)
comment "The transaction sort type describes all possible Transaction
    sorts"
typedef ATTRIBUTEKIND ENUM (Original, Derived)
typedef STEPKIND ENUM (
  Initial, Request, Requested, Promise, Promised, Execute, Executed,
      State, Declare, Stated, Declared, Accept, Accepted,
  Decline, Declined, Quit, Quited, Reject, Rejected, Stop, Stopped,
  RevokeRequest, RevokedRequest, ...)
```

Listing 4.2. Type definitions

To prevent listing the whole notation in this paper we will summarise the element section of the DEMO 3 notation. The notation contains all DEMO 3 the elements, e.g. Actor, Entity Type, Attribute Type, Elementary Actor Role, Composite Actor Role, Transaction Kind, Aggregate Transaction Kind, and Transaction Process Step Kind. Special attention is needed for the Actor element as the DEMOSL does not specify this element. In the DEMO methodology the Actor-Function-Matrix [8, p.94] lists Actors that are linked to the Transaction Kinds. This Actor, as shown in listing 4.3, is not defined in the methodology but needs to be present to complete the connection between those concepts.

```
element Actor Actor37
    ( Name TEXT )
element "Transaction Kind" TransactionKind37
        ( Name TEXT
    , "Product Kind Name" TEXT
        , "Product Kind Formulation" TEXT
        , "Transaction Sort" TRANSACTIONSORT)
```

Listing 4.3. Elements

The connections within the model have been listed   [7] and a summary of those findings are shown in Sect. 4. All connections between elements can be specified with the *connection* keyword, as shown in listing 4.4, and these have been specified in the notation script file (Table 1).

To → From ↓	ETK	ATK	EAR	CAR	ET	AT	CET	TPSK	AR
ETK	–	c	e	ce	–	–	–	–	–
ATK	–	–	–	–	–	–	–	–	–
EAR	ia	a	–	c	–	–	–	–	–
CAR	ia	a	–	c	–	–	–	–	–
ET	o	–	–	–	xsrg	–	–	–	–
AT	o	–	–	–	p	–	–	-	–
CET	o	–	–	–	–	–	–	–	–
TPSK	c	–	–	–	–	–	-	iy	tlwh
AR	–	–	–	–	W	–	–	–	–

Table 1. Element Property Types

	Property Types	
[c] contained in	[o] concerns	[i] initiator
[e] executor	[a] access to bank	[s] specialisation
[r] aggregation	[g] generalisation	[t] then
[l] else	[w] while	[h] when
[W] with	[x] excludes	[y] wait
[f] role of	[p] attribute of	

```
connection Initiator Initiator37e from ElementaryActorRole37 to
    TransactionKind37
connection Initiator Initiator37c from CompositeActorRole37 to
    TransactionKind37
connection "Attribute of Entity" AttributeOfEntity37 from
    AttributeType37 to EntityType37
```

Listing 4.4. Connections

The representation of models can be done in several ways. The most common notations involve diagrams and tables. To be able to verify the model we need to know what elements can exist on a diagram. This restriction does not limit the elements present on the diagram necessarily, but does give information about the verification of a 'pure' diagram. We have named the diagram according to the methodology [1] and match the elements present on those diagrams as shown in listing 4.5. We have chosen to have the connections allowed on the diagram to be derived from the elements that are allowed on the diagram. We could add them to the diagram as connection restrictions in a later stage but no specific requirement was found that did not allow for more connection types on a diagram.

```
diagram "Organisation Construction Diagram"
    OrganisationConstructionDiagram37
comment "OCD"
toolbox ToolboxOCD37
contains ( ElementaryActorRole37, CompositeActorRole37,
    TransactionKind37, AggregateTransactionKind37 )
```

Listing 4.5. OCD diagram

Before we show the definition of tables, we first introduce rules of a model. We have defined a grammar that mimics SQL and first order logic. Instead of adopting a complex specification language for rules we have started in a simplistic way to allow for the most common restrictions in a language. We have adopted the mathematical expressions 'for all', 'not exist' and 'exists' together with the logical 'and', 'or' and 'not'. The notation uses the mathematical representations of these terms (e.g. $\forall$, $\exists$, $\wedge$, $\vee$, !) which will not show up in the presented listings. When the logical rule collides with the given model, the message is presented to the user as shown in listing 4.6.

```
rule "No Reverse Association" (A connection Association(x, y) => !E
    connection Association(y, x))
Message "There can be no reverse association between two elements"
```

Listing 4.6. Rules

The same logical listing for rules is used in tables. This makes it possible to describe the table representation of a repository, model or diagram in a tabular format. This version has a one-dimensional representation where future versions are likely to have multi-dimensional representations allowing for more complex representation of model aspects like the Actor-Function-Table of DEMO.

```
table "Transaction Product Table" TransactionProductTable37
select (x."Identification",x."Name",x."Product Kind",x."Product Kind
    Formulation")
  (A element(x): x.Identification == "TransactionKind37")
column "transaction kind" span 2 data S0
column "tName" span 0 data S1
column "product kind" span 2 data S2
column "pName" span 0 data S3
```

Listing 4.7. TPT table

5   DEMO 4 Notation

The definition of the DEMO 4 notation has been derived from the notation of DEMO 3 in Sect. 4. DEMO 4 has an extra diagram notation compared to DEMO 3. DEMO4 also has some new connections that were not present in DEMO 3.

We will skip the parts of the notation specification that are the same as the DEMO 3 specification and show the DEMO 4 specific parts.

The elements of DEMO 4 are the same, but the names represent the DEMO 4 version, as shown in listing 5.1. The naming of some elements have changed like Aggregate Transaction Kind becomes Multiple Transaction Kind.

```
element EntityType EntityType40
        ( Identification TEXT
        , "Composite Entity" BOOL default "false" )
```

Listing 5.1. Element

The most challenging element is the Transactor. The transactor is the contraction of the Transaction Kind (TK) and the Elementary Actor Role (EAR), when these two elements are connected by an executor connection. In Fig. 1 we show a part of the metamodel of DEMO4 from DEMOSL 4.6.1. Furthermore, in the book [3], the diagram OCD is no longer discussed but the author has made it clear that DEMO 3 is still a valid notation. Additionally, we can read in the text on page 28 [3]: "Note that a transactor role is the combination of a transaction kind and the actor role that has its executor role.".

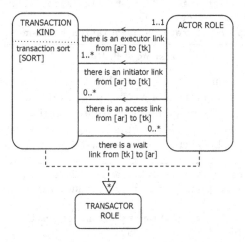

Fig. 1. DEMO 4 metamodel on transactor [3]

The Coordination Structure Diagram (CSD) has been introduced to emphasise the tree structures in the construction and to show the transactors that form business processes together. That being said, we could be visualising a demo model in a OCD and a CSD simultaneously. In the OCD, the TK - executor - EAR are represented by an element - connection - element. In the CSD this construction is represented by a single element that has multiple parts. The upper part of the visual notation is the TK and the lower part is the EAR. But the element would be a single element on the diagram. To accomplish this we have created a virtual element. A virtual element is the combination of n+1 elements that are connected by n connections in a single line. On the one hand, when this combination of elements and connections start to exist the virtual element starts to exist. In addition, a virtual element that is created will create the underlying components simultaneously. On the other hand, when one of the components of the virtual element is removed from the model, the virtual element will cease to exist. Similarly, removing a virtual element will remove all of its components. In listing 5.2 the Transactor is defined for DEMO 4.

```
virtual element Transactor Transactor40
  element TransactionKind40
  connection Executor4e
  element ElementaryActorRole40
```

Listing 5.2. Virtual element

We could have solved this notation behaviour of a CSD with the behaviour statement of Sect. 6, but this virtual element concept can have some benefits for other notations in the future.

The TPT in DEMO4, as shown in listing 5.3, has a different meaning because the first letter is taken from the Transactor. Therefore, this table has a new definition in the notation.

```
table "Transactor Product Table" TransactionProductTable40
select (x."Name",x."Identification",x."Product Kind",x."Product Kind
    Formulation",z."Identification",z."Name")
( A element(x): x.elementname == "TransactionKind40"
=> E connection(y): y.Source == x.Id AND y.connectionName == "
    Executor"
=> E element(z): y.Target == z.Id AND z.refname == "
    ElementaryActorRole40"
)
column "transaction kind" span 2 data S0
column "tName" span 0 data S1
column "product kind" span 2 data S2
column "pName" span 0 data S3
column "executor role" span 2 data S4
column "eName" span 0 data S5
```

Listing 5.3. TPT table

6   Notation Visualisation

Visualisation of models is a broader problem. In this paper we will keep the scope to the representation of model elements within a diagram representation of the model concepts. After defining the model concepts, we can define visualisations for these concepts. This visualisation is done by using a visual script which can contain a number of statements as described below. A visual script starts with an initialSizeStatement, specifying how large the objects should appear on the screen. Next, there are two possibilities. The first possibility is specifying penWidth, penColor, fillColor, and lineStyle, and subsequently defining a shape. The second possibility is using a groupStatement, which bundles together shapes defined within it. There are two types of groups, scaling, and non scaling. Scaling groups scale when the object would be scaled. Non-scaling groups do not scale and can be made by adding the noscale keyword, which is useful in certain cases such as text. Groups can contain other groups, but only if they are the same type, e.g. scale or noscale. Next, it is possible to define the shape that should be visualised. There are several basic shapes, and a free shape. We have a limited set of basic shapes, e.g. line, arc, polygon, rectangle and ellipse. The free shape can receive basic shapes, and will connect those to form one single closed shape. For these shapes, it is possible to define a minimum size using a minimumSizeStatement. Additionally, it is possible to display text, which is achieved using a printStatement.

Furthermore, there is the possibility of conditional visualisation using switch. The if statement can be accomplished by using a switch with a single case, since the default case is not required.

A certain concept can have multiple visualisations for multiple diagrams. This enables the modeller to define separate visuals for concepts such as a transaction kind, which has a different visualisation on an OCD compared to a Process Structure Diagram (PSD). Is is possible for an element to be visualised the same on all diagrams by substituting the diagramName by a star (*). In the model layer the visualisation of an element can occur multiple times on the same diagram.

In Simplified, the canvas has the positive x-axis to the right, and the positive y-axis down. Each grid square is 50×50 by default.

To accommodate the combination of the diagram and the elements and connections that can be on that diagram, the notation script can define the related elements and connections. The toolbox then can be presented to the user at the right moment while modelling. Though the toolbox shows the most likely options, other elements can be used in a notation when the diagram does not have to be pure for the methodology.

```
toolbox "OCD" ToolboxOCD37
comment "Toolbox with all elements for the OCD diagram"
(
  element TransactionKind37, element AggregateTransactionKind37,
  element ElementaryActorRole37, element CompositeActorRole37,
  connection Initiator37e, connection Initiator37c,
  connection Executor37e, connection Executor37c,
  connection Information37e, connection Information37c
)
```

Listing 6.1. Toolbox

In earlier versions of DEMO [1] the fact model has been modelled in a different notation. This former notation was closer to Object Role Modelling (ORM) and allowed for the attributes of entities to be modelled as elements in the fact model. The advantage of modelling attributes of entities as separate elements is the ability to reason about them. Connections to separated attributes can be made not only to the entity by the connection type 'attribute of entity' but also to other concepts. In order to model both earlier and current versions of DEMO, attributes can be visually modelled both as attributes of entities and as elements themselves while still using the same notation for the non-visual model.

The Action Rules Specification (ARS) is a concept that needs further research in itself. The complexity of action rules is bigger than a simple representation can visualise. Therefore, within this scope we just stick to the structure and a simple representation. For the ARS the 'with' specification [7] refers to attributes of entities. The connection from the 'when', 'then' and 'else' proposition to all relevant attributes can now be visually modelled and translated to a verbalisation and vise-versa. The visual challenge is to create a behaviour of the attribute element when it 'belongs' graphically to the entity. We have created the behaviour syntax to be able to define just that behaviour. This behaviour is of the same kind as the placing of activities on a swim-lane in a Business Process Model and Notation (BPMN) diagram.

```
behaviour "Attribute on Entity" on drop AttributeType37 on
    EntityType37
do link AttributeType37 to EntityType37
option align left,centre
```

Listing 6.2. Behaviour

Drawing all shapes of DEMO requires just a few mathematical basic shapes. The behaviour of these shapes, thought not all explicitly defined in DEMOSL 4.6.1, is quite challenging. We have decided to start with the basic set of figures and text that allows for defining the required shapes. The resizing of the transaction kind shape on a PSD is not yet optimised but will do the job in this first version. The conditional statements allow for changing the colour based on properties of the diagram or the element.

```
visualscript: initialSizeStatement vscrStatement* ;
visualScriptSettingStatements: vscrSSStatement* ;
vscrSSStatement:
      penWidthStatement  |  penColorStatement
    | fillColorStatement | lineStyleStatement

    ;
vscrStatement:
      minimumSizeStatement | penWidthStatement
    | penColorStatement  |  fillColorStatement
    | lineStatement  |       arcStatement
    | anchorStatement |      polygonStatement
    | rectangleStatement | ellipseStatement
    | printStatement  |      groupStatement
    | switchStatement |      lineStyleStatement
    | letStatement  |        shapeStatement

    ;
```

Listing 6.3. Visual Grammar

The listing listing 6.4 is an example of the response link on a PSD. It will start with a circle and follows a solid line to the end of the connection with a rectangle at the end. All connection visualisations can have a line, begin, centre and end part as shown in Fig. 2 and Fig. 3.

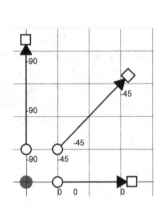

Fig. 2. Response link Simplified

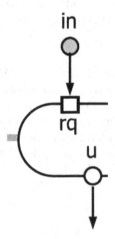

Fig. 3. Response link [3]

```
visual ResponseLinkPsd37 of ResponseLink37
on (ProcessStructureDiagram37)
   line {
        penwidth(2) / linestyle(solid)
        pencolor(0,0,0)
   }
   begin{
        initialsize(5,5) / fillcolor(255, 255, 255)
        ellipse(0, 0, 8, 8, 0)
   }
   end {
        initialsize(5,5) / fillcolor(0,0,0)
        polygon(0,0,3,10,90)
        fillcolor(255, 255, 255) / linestyle(solid)
        rectangle(10, -8, 15, 15, 0, 0)
   }
```

Listing 6.4. Visual Response link

For the preclusion connection, as shown in listing 6.5, a centre and end figure are used as shown in Fig. 4 and Fig. 5.

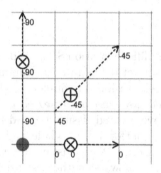

Fig. 4. Preclusion link Simplified

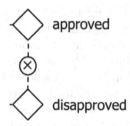

Fig. 5. Exclusion link [3]

```
visual PreclusionOfd37 of Preclusion37 on (ObjectFactDiagram37)
   line { penwidth(2)
     pencolor(0,0,0) / linestyle(dash) }
   centre { initialsize(5,5)     / linestyle(solid)
     ellipse(0,0,10,10,0)
     line(-6,-6,6,6,0) / line(-6,6,6,-6,0) }
   end { initialsize(5,5)     / penwidth(2)
     pencolor(0,0,0) / linestyle(solid)
     line(0, 0, -10, 5, 0) / line(0, 0, -10, -5, 0) }
```

Listing 6.5. Visual Preclusion

Elements also need a visualisation and the simplest visualisation is that of an EAR shown in listing 6.6. This is a square with the text in the square and some text beneath the square. As can be seen the graphical shapes will scale and the text will not scale along.

```
visual ElementaryActorRoleAll137 of ElementaryActorRole37 on (*)
{
  initialSize(50,50)
  group (0,0) scale {
    penWidth(2) / penColor(0,0,0)
    fillcolor(255,255,255) / rectangle(0,0,50,50,0,0)
  }
  group (0,0) noscale {
    print(10, 20, 40, 25, "{element.identification}", 0)
    print(-25, 60,100, 25, "{element.name}", 0)
  }
}
```

Listing 6.6. Visual EAR

All these visualisation concepts cover most of the CM, PM, FM but do not cover the AM fully yet.

7   Conclusion and Discussion

Creating a complete DEMO description in the Simplified Notation Script is on its way. Several aspects of the DEMO notation are not yet defined in the grammar of the notation script, but the main graphical representations are implementable in the notation. The notation script, as developed now, has been proved to be successful in the test model examples that we have created. Issues beyond the notationscript are withholding the release of the platform as a whole and do interfere with the public evaluation of the notationscript. Notwithstanding, this evaluation of the notationscript and its application shows that the first aspect model of DEMO can be successfully be created and used for practical modelling.

The notation will be enhanced in the coming period to accommodate all aspects of the DEMO notation. It is worth bearing in mind that the DEMO methodology comprises more than only the notation, e.g. process information. However, at this point in time we did not find a way to describe all this information in the notation script grammar. Therefore, some parts of the methodology support are still hard-coded until we have found a suitable way to describe the translation and generation of certain notation aspects.

The notation scripts will be published on a Git[1] to be used and improved by the community. This direct communication loop with the community will also benefit the specification of additional notations in Simplified in the future.

---

[1] https://gitlab.com/teec2/simplified/notations.

8   Future Research

During this attempt to describe DEMO in Simplified Notation Script we have come across several shortcomings that prevented us to be fully capable of modelling DEMO. First of all, the ARS grammar that was defined [7] is not included in the implementation yet and the visualisation of the ARS in an ARD is also not implemented yet either. Visualisation of the ARS is a subject that we will research further, parallel to the creation of the notation. Secondly, both the DEMO methodology and the aspect models with their specific visualisations make it quite challenging to make a solid definition to capture all concepts. Meaning that it will most likely be improved upon in the coming time. Lastly, compared to the hard-coded version of the DEMO modelling tool as an extension to SEA we still have to implement the generation options for the following diagrams: CSD, Transaction Pattern Diagram (TPD), Action Rules Process (ARP) and PSD.

Opportunities for improvement include the addition of a delete option to the notation script concepts as it currently supports only the definition, extension and replacement of the concepts. This would allow for a better accommodation of the language enhancements. Challenges of expanding the notation, and even connecting the notation to other notations are subjects that need more research.

Furthermore, the connection concept can be expanded upon. Currently, the grammar does not support multiple connections but the metamodel does support already n-ary connection. Although DEMO does not require n-ary connections in the current diagrams, we will have to extend the grammar to support this kind of connection for the addition of other diagrams and notations in the future. One of the concepts that needs the n-ary connections is the exclusion law in fact diagrams where two relations can be mutual exclusive.

We have only listed the research subjects of our R&D that are directly adjacent to the topic notation script.

References

1. Dietz, J.L.G.: Enterprise Ontology - Theory and Methodology. Springer, Heidelberg (2006). https://doi.org/10.1007/3-540-33149-2
2. Dietz, J.L.G., et al.: The discipline of enterprise engineering. Int. J. Organ. Design Eng. **3**(1), 86–114 (2013)
3. Dietz, J.L.G., Mulder, J.B.F.: Enterprise Ontology - A Human-Centric Approach to Understanding the Essence of Organisation. The Enterprise Engineering Series. Springer, Heidelberg (2020). https://doi.org/10.1007/978-3-030-38854-6
4. Dietz, J.L.G., Mulder, M.A.T.: Demo specification language 3.7 (2017)
5. Habermas, J.: The Theory for Communicative Action: Reason and Rationalization of Society, vol. 1. Boston Beacon Press, Boston (1984)
6. Mulder, M.A., Mulder, R., Bodnar, F., van Kessel, M., Gomez Vicente, J., et al.: The simplified platform, an overview. In: Modellierung 2022 Satellite Events (2022)
7. Mulder, M.: Enabling the automatic verification and exchange DEMO models. Ph.D. thesis, Radboud University Netherlands (2022)

8. Perinforma, A.P.C.: The Essence of Organisation, 3rd edn. Sapio, The Netherlands (2013)
9. van Reijswoud, V.E., Dietz, J.L.G.: DEMO Modelling Handbook, vol. 1, 2nd edn. Delft University of Technology (1999)
10. Wieringa, R.J.: Design Science Methodology for Information Systems and Software Engineering. Springer, Heidelberg (2014). https://doi.org/10.1007/978-3-662-43839-8

Towards DEMO Model-Based Automatic Generation of Smart Contracts

David Aveiro[1,2,3](✉) (iD) and João Oliveira[2,3] (iD)

[1] ARDITI - Regional Agency for the Development of Research, Technology and Innovation, 9020-105 Funchal, Portugal
`daveiro@uma.pt`
[2] NOVA-LINCS, Universidade NOVA de Lisboa, Campus da Caparica, 2829-516 Caparica, Portugal
`joliveira@staff.uma.pt`
[3] University of Madeira, Caminho da Penteada, 9020-105 Funchal, Portugal

Abstract. The production of self-executing computational agreements in the form of smart contracts remains a manual coding endeavour that hinders the widespread adoption of solutions that run on top of a distributed ledger technology such as blockchain. We explore the automatic generation of smart contracts based on a visual composition of reusable action rule specifications and other elements from the action model of the DEMO methodology. Several design and implementation considerations entail this choice of SC generation, all of which motivated a smart contract-enabled extension of DEMO's way of modelling. The main research contribution is a foundation of synergistic knowledge accompanied by an extension proposal involving DEMO and smart contracts that can be built upon in future business cases where enterprise interoperability supported by blockchain technology is a requirement.

Keywords: Smart contracts · Enterprise engineering · DEMO · Action model · Action rule specification

1 Introduction

The evolution of Distributed Ledger Technology (DLT) popularized solutions such as blockchain that promise a distributed, decentralized, synchronized and consensual database [1]. A smart contract is a self-executing, autonomous program that runs on top of blockchain. Its terms are coded to satisfy the interests of involved parties who may not have a foundation of trust in their relationship [2]. A central mediating authority and its inherent costs and inefficiencies are, therefore, avoided because the contract is immutable, its execution irreversible and automated throughout all of the nodes of the constituting ledger.

In the context of the DEMO methodology, of the EE field of knowledge, there have been recent advances in synergizing elements from its essential models, mainly the Construction and Action Models, with proof-of-concept smart contract implementations that leverage BC as a notarization and transaction execution system [3–5]. However,

C. Griffo et al. (Eds.): EEWC 2022, LNBIP 473, pp. 71–89, 2023.
https://doi.org/10.1007/978-3-031-34175-5_5

current research landscape of smart contract generation from DEMO models (or even models from other modeling languages) still leads to a situation where the production of contracts is a mostly manual coding endeavor that handicaps the potential of DLTs in the implementation of a DEMO based information systems [6, 7].

Despite these advances, we consider that there is room to evolve the DEMO specification language so that we might have automatically generated DEMO-based smart contracts, with minimal need of manual coding or even none at all. In fact, recent studies [8, 9] have proven that there is potential in DEMO extensions that, although not semantically equivalent as, for instance, DEMO v4.5 [10], are still capable of capturing the essence of an organization. It seems that these extensions can provide a holistic view that not only accommodates BC integration, but also reaps the communicational benefits of being brought closer to the lingo of business practitioners. Taking this into account, the following research question is formulated in this paper: - Can DEMO's Specification Language be extended in order to support a more complete automatic generation of DEMO-based smart contracts?

Throughout this paper, and whenever it is opportune, we will resort to the mortgage case described in [7] to illustrate the points that are being conveyed in the alternative DEMO version proposed in [11, 12].

2   Literature Review

In order to situate the innovation of our approach, this section briefly presents the current research landscape of DEMO's action rule specification (ARS) languages and of the generation of smart contracts based on business rules and domain representations.

2.1   DEMO's Action Model

The operation of an organization is addressed in the DEMO methodology through its Action Model [13]. For each of the transaction coordination facts of the transaction pattern [14], an action rule can be produced, which specifies the guidelines that the actors must comply with whilst fulfilling their respective business roles. Actors are still allowed to deviate from expected behavior and autonomously decide and do the work from their agenda based on their professional and general knowledge [13].

DEMO's standard for Action Rule Specification (ARS) language have evolved through time, starting with a pseudo-algorithmic language [15] and culminating, in DEMO's specification language 4.5, in a definition which adheres to the Extended Backus-Naur Form (EBNF) [10]. In it's latest version, an ARS is tripartite: - The event part specifies which coordination events are responded to by means of a set clauses; - The assess part, by being based on Habermas' theory of communicative action, holds a set of validity claims that must be determined to be true with respect to the rightness, sincerity and truth conditions of the world; - And the final part, the response, which consists of a mandatory if clause that specifies what action has to be taken if advancing is considered to be justifiable, and, otherwise, in an optional else clause, the possible accountable actions that can be taken by the executing actor if he autonomously deems an exceptional situation to be justifiable [13].

Andrade et al. [16], proposed an alternative ARS language for the Action Model, also in EBNF, whilst advocating its suitability for the implementation of an action rule engine and the execution of action models (and its ARSs) in a live production setting. According to this approach, as in DEMO's latest AM version, the execution of an AR, for a particular transaction state, is triggered by its corresponding coordination event (e.g. request, promise, etc.) and multiple other actions may follow by means of causal links. However, by also considering expressions, logical conditions, validations, input forms, and templated-document outputs in the EBNF, which are constructs closer to an actual information system, it is argued that the alternative ARS language circumvents the unnecessary faults, complexities and ambiguities introduced by the so-called "structured english" sentences of DEMO's tripartite claim-based syntax.

2.2 Smartcontract Generation Based on Business Rules and Domain Representations

Blockchain technologies have the inherent capability of recording in a distributed ledger of encrypted blocks, a set of transactions involving multiple parties. Because the ledger is maintained in a distributed manner, the proposal of a new block contains a cryptographic hash of the previous block and has to be broadcasted and consensualized by the network of peer participants who keep their own copy of the immutable, time stamped ledger [17]. Self-executing computational agreements in the form of smart contracts can also be run on top of a blockchain. The digital execution of agreed-upon smart contractual terms enable enterprise interoperability in collaborative business processes without the need, or cost, of an external trust authority.

Choudhury et al. [6] resort to ontologies and semantic rules to encode domain-specific knowledge and leverage an intermediate abstract syntax tree (AST) whose traversal yields the source code file for the smart contract to be produced. In a transaction-focused system, and because translating business rules to smart contracts requires time and technical proficiency, there is added reusability value in ontology-driven smart contract templates that have the capability to capture all possible manifestations of the domain at hand in terms of its classes, properties and relationships. An instance of a smart contract can then be automatically generated from the traversal of the AST representation of the template whilst combining its business rules and constraints with dynamic values of instance-specific settings.

Hornackova et al., explore possible synergies between smart contracts and DEMO models for the purpose of building blockchain-enabled enterprise information systems (EIS) for decentralized autonomous organizations (DAOs) [5]. Specifically, and in the context of the DEMO methodology, a smart contract could be interpreted as a border transaction whose C-Acts of its underlying transaction pattern seamlessly overlap with the set of immutable commitments that are agreed upon with an external actor or third-party EIS. By representing a coordination point at the "border" of the world of interest, a smart contract can conveniently notarize not only documents and data from DEMO (meta-)models, but also information regarding the trustless execution of the transactions of business processes. The identified principles, synergies, implementation details and trade-off decisions are accompanied with a proposal for an EIS architecture based on DEMO and BC.

Aparício et al. [3, 4] rely on the reported advantages of the MDE approach to implement DEMO's AM directly into automatically generated SCs. It is advocated that the AM is a prime candidate for creation of SCs as it stands at the base and includes all elements of all the other integrated DEMO aspect models as shown in Fig. 1.

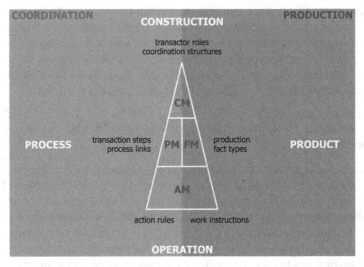

Fig. 1. Ontological aspect models [13]

As such, it is shown how the AM, and specifically its ARSs, by containing all the detailed elements of the other models, can be directly mapped to the structure and content of a SC and thus be used to directly generate its software production code. The implementation of DEMO's AM with SCs is also shown to entail some ontological, infological and datalogical considerations. It is suggested that the automation that SCs bring forth can suppress the need for some trust-related transaction types which become tacitly performed by the BC. However, because only human subjects can be responsible for transactions at performa, informa, and forma levels, the co-existence of human subjects with the BC is not deemed to be at risk. Although a SC can assume the form of an agent, it cannot deal autonomously with ontological P-acts and, as such, the authors present a solution where the explicit declaration of a transaction with the invocation of the SC function that represents the "declare" C-act can assist in tacitly "performing" the P-acts. Implementation-wise, in Solidity SCs, the P-act can be represented by a function modifier, i.e. a dedicated precondition that executes and guards against unintended invocations of the contract function that represents the transaction declaration. An event is then emitted to interested parties corresponding to the P-fact result [4].

Motivated to make automatic smart contract generation from EE-based models, Skotnica and Pergl's [7] approach intends to avoid the possibility of coding mistakes, semantic ambiguities and loss of expressiveness by means of a high-level visual modelling language. A smart contract is described through a combination of 4 visual DEMO and BPMN models which extend the reach of contract specification to "non-technical people".

3 Project Context

Recent advances in the logistics knowledge area, brought forth the concept of micro-hubs where participants such as express and freight forwarders collaborate in a network of strategically-placed logistic centers in order to reliably deliver the parcels under their responsibility whilst accomplishing commercial and environmental sustainability goals. By having resources shared and optimized among logistical operators, an improved quality of service and a wider geographical coverage can be achieved without a significant increase in operating costs and initial investments.

The recognized advantages of adhering to collaborative micro-hubs are still dependent however on a credible technological solution that, at its core, inherently addresses the inter-organizational trust issues when data is exchanged following the execution of logistical operations.

This paper is driven by a micro-hubs project - MiColEC (Micro-hubs Colaborativos para a Economia Circular) - which proposes to leverage Blockchain technology to implement a robust and reliable digital solution that solves the collaboration and trust issues that typically inhibit the participation of new players in collaborative micro-hubs. Smart contracts in particular have the potential to register all transactions of the micro-hub, i.e. of the express couriers, producers, end consumers and recycling centers, etc. in a verifiable, permanent and transparent way to all interested logistical agents [22, 23].

Tallyn et al. [20], conducted a logistics hubs case study composed of 4 urban delivery scenarios (Person-to-Person, Hub-to-Person, Person-to-Hub and Hub-to-Hub) coordinated by smart-contracts, involving professionals in their existing work practices. It reflects on the delicate balance between the increased automation, coordination, efficiency and accountability brought by SC-mediated last-mile deliveries and the omission of social connections from which trust is traditionally built on between couriers and receptionists when hubs and lock-boxes are introduced.

Influenced by blockchain-design leveraged by the TOVE traceability ontology, Kim & Laskowsky [21] developed smart contracts, whose execution intends to track physical resources and their provenance along inter-organizational, internationally-spanning supply chains. with respect to the ontological traceability constraints that are enforced upon the distributed ledger.

However, and despite the potential already demonstrated, the current literature on the application of blockchain to collaborative micro-hubs is limited to analyzing the type of requirements and factors that play a role in this specific system of logistics collaboration. A viable practical solution for a collaborative micro-hub network needs to respond to the logistics needs of circular economy processes in a system with incentives for participation. For this purpose, a prototype blockchain-based platform that can confirm the market potential of the proposed concept is to be implemented to support the generation and execution of smart contracts between express couriers, end consumers, producers, collection and recycling centers which operate in a network of collaborative micro-hubs.

3.1 Research Methodology

For this project, the design-science research is an appropriate fit because the production of novel and innovative artifacts, in this case the method for automatically generating smart contracts from DEMO models and the computational tools that they entail, brings forth an opportunity to expand the boundaries of existing theory whilst iteratively understanding the design problem at hand and the solution for logistics collaboration.

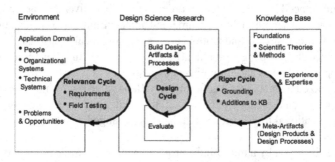

For that effect, the Seven Guidelines for Design Science in Information Systems Research [24] were followed and the executed Design Science Research Cycles [25] will be summarily disclosed as follows. The Relevance cycle had to be addressed with care as stakeholders had to be guaranteed to not be competing in the application domain of the project which is last-mile delivery. In this domain, the competition is deflated due to the lack of appeal for reduced profit margins and optimized field operations. In turn, this constituted an opportunity for logistics collaboration while being leveraged by the technical virtues of smart contracts. However, the technicalities of smart contracts raise barriers in terms of the expertise, time and effort needed in producing such a contract and thus it is a relevant requirement to fulfil. The design artifacts, i.e. the DEMO (meta)-models, computational tools and generated smart contracts were subjected to rapid iterations of the Design Cycle and assessed until the designed method allowed the production of smart contracts matching the contracts' code and semantics of an already established Mortgage case [7]. This paper builds upon existing knowledge, namely the EE theories and the DEMO methodology and it is in the Rigor Cycle that our contribution to the community is established. From the soundness of the EE-theories, the newly proposed DEMO artifacts were and will still be subjected to Design Science Research Cycles whose outcome will be published in future scientific releases.

4 Proposed Solution

There are recent proposals for new representations of DEMO's essential models [11, 12], where it is argued that these should be aligned, not only with the lingo of business practitioners, but selectively with concrete implementation details that entail meta-model additions and modifications in alternative DEMO extensions.

4.1 SC-Enabled Process Model

In the coordination world of an organization, the PM connects the CM and the AM, in regards to the state and transition spaces. The representation of the state space by means of a PSD shows all internal and border transaction kinds, the process step kinds as well as the applicable existence laws [13]. Likewise, for the PM's transition space, it must be taken into consideration that there are relationships between DEMO transactions, as manifested through the PSD via response and waiting links.

It is consistent across literature [3–5] that implementing DEMO-based SCs requires a direct mapping between the DEMO's meta-model elements and the constructs that are made available by SC programming languages such as Solidity [18]. This mapping constitutes a set of premises that are assumed when discussing the implementation details of SCs. These are summarily presented as follows:

1. A SC instance should be taken per DEMO transaction instance [7];
2. DEMO's finite set of all c-facts from the transaction pattern may be specified as an enumeration in the SC [3, 19];
3. Each c-act corresponds to an invocable contract method that is built from its associated ARS and changes the contract's state to the respective c-fact. The nomenclature for SC methods is composed of the c-act followed by the transaction's name, e.g. requestRentalCompletion [4];
4. Interested parties, like external EIS, that depend on the SC's execution (e.g. state change to a specific c-fact), are notified with an event [5];
5. The p-act may be implemented through a function modifier that is only called in functions that represent the coordination act "declare". The function modifier that represents the p-act will emit an event corresponding to the p-fact, as a production fact is the result of performing a production act [3, 4];
6. SC-enabled DEMO transactions are typically border transactions [5];
7. Enclosed transactions with response and waiting links may be considered as a separate referenceable contract, inside the enclosing contract or left outside of the BC altogether [5];

It is evident from this set of premises that the impact of SC implementation, if it were to be expressed in DEMO's models, would not only change the representation of the PM, but also span throughout several of DEMO representations in the CM, FM and specifically the ARSs of the AM.

In order to convey these SC motivated changes in a clear and concise manner, for the purpose of this paper, the PM representation that will be adopted includes the PSD version proposed in [11]. This representation fuses part of the contents of DEMO's Process, Cooperation, and Action models towards a more agile and comprehensive solution to depict the essence of the organizational reality [8]. This PSD representation has the added convenience of being capable of visually expressing important SC-related semantics that will be described in the following paragraphs. As such, and whenever it is pertinent, changes to the PSD meta-elements of Fig. 2 will be illustrated.

As discussed in [5], besides being capable of being interpreted as a DEMO transaction, a smart contract can also represent a coordination point between an internal EIS (e.g. a DEMO machine) and external actors. When it comes to border transactions, it should be made clear in its representation that a transaction kind is leveraged by blockchain. A new "smart transaction kind" involving a non-internal actor role is presented in Fig. 3 with the corresponding adornment as an extension for DEMO v4.5.

Moreover, and implementation-wise, border transactions may imply an integration development between two EIS. It becomes justifiable to distinguish smart transaction

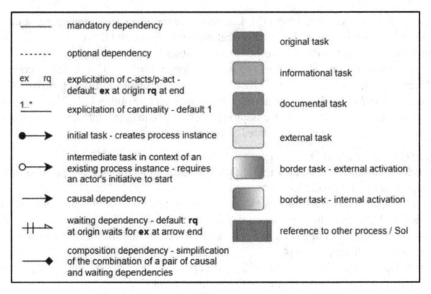

Fig. 2. Alternative PSD meta-elements from [11]

Fig. 3. A smart-border transaction kind

kinds from "regular" border transaction kinds with the corresponding adornment because the integration effort can be decentralized and "hosted" in the blockchain with a trustless execution of transactions. The ontological implications that follow this sort of usage of SCs are also discussed in [4].

Elaborating on premise 7, it should be taken into account, when representing DEMO-based SCs at the PM level, that it is not enough to only consider whether enclosed transactions are implemented as a separate referenceable contract, inside the enclosing contract or left outside of the BC.

The combination of these possibilities along with the PSD meta-elements from [11] yields several reusable model fragments of interest. Because it is not within the scope of this paper to explore all the possibilities of combinations, a couple of model fragments which were deemed to be reuse-worthy are described as follows.

In a composition of 1..* sub-smart transactions as shown in Fig. 4, each sub-smart transaction is created and an SC address is returned in order for both involved parties of both transactions to engage in a business conversation which is ruled by the SC's implementation and mediated by the transaction pattern.

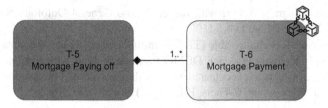

Fig. 4. A composition of 1..* smart transaction kind

Several details surface. For instance, the parent smart transaction has to keep track of its sub-smart transactions. Also, and if there are sub-smart transactions of different types/kinds involved in the composition itself, waiting links may be implemented as function modifiers that guard against unintended invocations of the waiting transaction's c-acts and causal links may be implemented as a function invocation to the sub-SC as a consequence of performing a certain C-act [4, 5].

Another possible reusable model fragment of interest is a composition of a smart transaction with a smart-enclosed documental task where only some steps of the transaction pattern are performed on the blockchain and, as such, without the need of a separate contract. For this purpose, a square surrounding the smart contract adornment is represented in the documental task of Fig. 5.

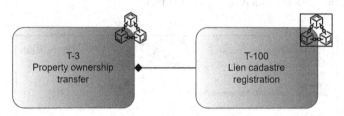

Fig. 5. A composition of a smart transaction with a smart-enclosed documental task

Smart transactions can be leveraged to achieve a certain level of automation by letting SCs behave autonomously as agents and perform C-acts as tacitly as possible without compromising the authority and responsibilities of the executing actor's role [4]. In this manner, and taking premise 5 into account, "declaring" (C-act) a smart-enclosed documental transaction can conveniently be used as a means to support information notarization (e.g. documents) and knowledge sharing between actors which are notified via subscribable BC events [5, 7].

4.2 DEMO's Fact Model

In the production world of an organization, the FM connects the CM and the AM, in regards to the state and transition spaces. The products of an organization, i.e. all the identified entity types, value types, property types, attribute types, and event types accompanied by applicable existence laws and occurrence laws, are conveyed through the Object Fact Diagram (OFD) with respect to the General Ontology Specification Language (GOSL) of DEMO v4.5 [10].

A Transaction Blockchain Table (TBT) is introduced in [5] and specifies BC implementation details by mapping each DEMO transaction kind with the list of facts to notarize, the list of C-acts to execute and whether the execution of the transaction should be notarized (i.e. the C-Acts, C-Facts, P-facts, …) as shown in Fig. 6.

Transaction	Fact notarization	Transaction notarization	Execution
Transaction kind	List of facts to notarize	Yes/No	List of C-Acts to execute

Fig. 6. The Transaction Blockchain Table Template [5]

Just like the TBT, the Fact Description Table (FDT) from the notation presented in [12], is a cross-model representation which specifies information from the Construction and Fact aspect models, namely the transaction kinds that create or update value for the facts' properties. A novel version for the FDT should also include the list of facts to notarize. A FDT sample for the "Ownership Transferred Property" fact from the mortgage case is presented in Fig. 7. As mentioned in [12], a concept is to be interpreted as a fact and an attribute as a property of that fact.

Concept	Attribute name	Value Type	Referenced Concept / Category values	Source - task 1	Step	Task 1 (creates or updates the attribute)	Notarize?	Oracle?
Ownership Transferred Property	Ownership Transferred Property			Mortgage case	Ex	T3 - Property ownership transfer	☑	☐
Ownership Transferred Property	New owner	reference	Person	Mortgage case	Rq	T3 - Property ownership transfer	☐	☐
Ownership Transferred Property	Lein	document		Mortgage case	Rq	T3 - Property ownership transfer	☑	☐
Ownership Transferred Property	Amount to pay	number		Mortgage case	Rq	T3 - Property ownership transfer	☑	☐

Fig. 7. Expanded Fact Description Table with BC

It can be argued, in comparison with the TBT, that the addition of a granular representation of attributes in the table is relevant from a notarization standpoint because not all of attributes of a certain concept might be of interest in a SC. When it comes to querying external data, Ethereum oracles provides a convenient interface between SCs and the outside world [5]. Facts and attributes that are to be made available in accordance with Ethereum's[1] oracle design pattern should also be flagged. For that effect, not only the FDT, but also the Concept Attribute Diagram (CAD) of [12] can conveniently help in identifying, with the proper attribute granularity, what belongs to an oracle. Samples for the FDT and the CAD are presented in Fig. 7 and Fig. 8 respectively.

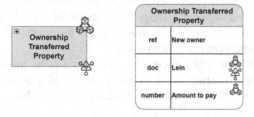

Fig. 8. Collapsed and expanded Concept Attribute Diagram

4.3 DEMO's Action Model

The crux of our solution lies in using an updated proposal of an ARS language, which allows a semantically richer and formal specification of logical and mathematical expressions and flow control of business rules, essential for less error prone smart contracts [16]. The specification of these rules (see Fig. 9) can be done in a visual programming language, thus allowing a more effective participation of non technically savvy collaborators.

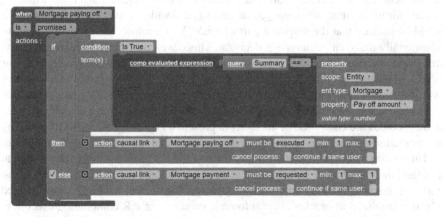

Fig. 9. Action rule for the promise of the "Mortgage completion" transaction

Because the proposed ARS language also supports constructs/rules with references to features like smart contracts, documents, templates, etc., the essential models placed

---

[1] https://ethereum.org/

on top of the AM are consequently affected like previously shown and their derived implementation is brought closer to an actual EIS.

In the following paragraphs, and due to size limitations, some key excerpts from a recent, yet to publish, new version of ARS language will be presented with an accompanying explanation. The choice of excerpts is based on whether the contained rules are of interest to be compiled/implemented into a SC in a production setting.

At the root of the language, i.e. in the production rule for the "when" terminal symbol (see Table 1), it is discernible that an action occurs in the context of a transaction type in the activation of a particular transaction state.

Regarding DEMO-based SC specification, the first novelty introduced by the ARS language is a dual specification of ARs for each activated transaction state: - for the acts; - and for the facts. This duality is discriminated in the following production rules excerpt of Table 1 by the IS and HAS-BEEN keywords:

Table 1. EBNF excerpt for WHEN clause

when	WHEN transaction_type IS|HAS-BEEN transaction_state {action} -
transaction_state	REQUESTED | (…) | REVOKE_ACCEPTANCE_REFUSED
action	causal_link | assign_expression | user_input | edit_entity_instance | user_output | produce_doc | if | while | foreach

In this manner, once a transaction state "HAS-BEEN" achieved/performed, the facts and "user_input"(e.g. obtained via user filled forms) that are important, in the scope of the transaction instance at hand, are guaranteed to have been created and made available in order for the contract to behave as an agent and decide its next course of action. It should be noticed that the response part of DEMO v4.5 allows the executing actor to exceptionally make an autonomous decision. This deviating behavior clearly contrasts with the contractual nature of SCs and should not be allowed. This dual specification for each C-act changes premise 3, to the following: - Each C-act corresponds to a couple of invocable contract methods that are built from their associated ARS and changes the contract's state to the respective C-fact after the first method invocation. The nomenclature for SC methods are composed of the C-act in present and past verbal forms followed by the transaction's name, e.g. requestRentalCompletion and requestedRentalCompletion;

This duality also underlines the importance of the FDT since it makes explicit what facts (and their attributes) are supposed to be available on a per transaction type basis. Moreover, because the FDT offers a thorough specification of which facts are flagged to be decentralized as oracles, their automatic creation via AR compilation/execution, whether in an EIS, SC and/or Oracle, becomes FDT-mediated. Table 1 also shows production rules for C-facts that are encoded as an enumeration structure in the SC as stated in premise 2.

Regarding facts that contain documents, the FM version, that the FDT is part of, conveniently reserves the "doc" and the "doc & text" value types for attributes. These can be effectively used to specify the documental attributes that should be notarized in the SC whenever its corresponding transaction is instantiated. The production of the documents is specified in the EBNF rules of Table 2:

Table 2. EBNF excerpt with rules for document templates

produce_doc	static_template I form_template I doc_attr_template
static_template	STRING NOTE: special HTML code annotated with custom directives which a PDF is generated
form_template	STRING NOTE: special HTML code annotated with custom directives from which a PDF is generated. The interpretation of some directives in this rule prompts the end-user at runtime for additional input (e.g. an observation to be placed in the PDF)
doc_attr_template	STRING NOTE: A reference to previously stored special HTML code annotated with custom directives from which a PDF is generated

These rules assume the existence of a templating component that leverages the generation of PDF documents. Templates are designed in a WYSIWYG editor where special HTML code is annotated with custom directives that inject data from the essential models directly into the final PDF when the templating engine is run. Because the interpretation of some directives may prompt the end-user for additional input, another moment should be taken into account besides the design time of the template. At runtime, when a document is about to be produced, a form is rendered to complete the information required by the templating engine (e.g. an observation or even more data from the essential models). These two moments are distinguished in the "static_template" and "form_template" rules. According to the "doc_attr_template", a document may already have been generated, persisted and stored, for which a reference is enough to retrieve it. In the context of BC, the immutability of data can be leveraged to certify different stages of business processes that are supported by documents of official value. In this manner, the specification of ARs in such processes may include actions that notarize documents. Such documents can effectively constitute a proof (e.g. with digital signatures) that a particular event has taken place and stored in the blockchain, either directly, or with a respective immutable hash of it.

Elaborating on [5], the TBT maintains which c-acts are to be executed in the BC. This information may be used to instruct the traversal of the AST in order for the AR engine to either: - execute the ARs at runtime; - or to preemptively generate the source code of a SC function corresponding to a particular c-act when a transaction is created. In this manner, if the c-act is present in the TBT, then the second case applies. The EBNF rules that are related to causal links are presented in Table 3.

One very important aspect of our approach is that we are adopting an evolved Action Meta-Model which includes the possibility of specifying actions of kind: if-then-else

Table 3. EBNF excerpt for causal links

causal_link	transaction_type MUST BE transaction_state [min [max]] [CANCEL_PROC] [CONTINUE_IF_SAME_USER]
transaction_type	STRING NOTE: has to be a transaction specified in the system
min	Integer
max	Integer | *

statements with specification of complex logical expressions; as well as value assignment to (possibly notarized) attributes, which might include also complex mathematical expressions. Table 4 presents the main expression production rules, Fig. 10 illustrates the visual ARS for the declaration of the "Mortgage payment" according to our proposal and, likewise, in Fig. 11 the ARS in DEMO v4.5.

Table 4. Characterization of the sample

assign_expression	property "=" (term | property_value)
property	STRING
term	constant | value | property | query | compute_expression

This also enables the possibility of a direct translation of business logic with complex logical and mathematical rules to smart contract code that executes such logical expression. The fact that these complex business logic rules can easily be interpreted and validated by business people, thanks to the Blockly based GUI to design and represent ARS, allows an early and important validation step by business people, which will, we expect, reduce the probability of mistakes and error exploitation in BC based SCs.

5   Discussion and Future Work

Our approach is a relevant evolution of the state-of-the-art regarding generation of smart contracts from DEMO based models. We can produce a finer grained set of rules for converting model elements into smart contracts code, greatly reducing the need to manually program them, which is prone to possible errors and exploits. Comparing Figs. 10 and 11, we can see how our approach allows a graphically friendly (and syntax protected) definition of action rules in a Blockly GUI with additional details on how to use parameters, properties, links to other c-facts or calculations, all of which are closer to a direct mapping to the programming constructs of the solidity language thus facilitating a transpilation via an AST. On the other hand, the standard DEMO approach, whose constructs are still derived from a semi-structured natural language, leads to an ambiguous specification of action rules which may erroneously translate to solidity code that does not reflect the terms of the contract to be executed. The solidity function which is expected to be generated from the ARS of the mortgage case is presented in the following code listing with minor corrections:

```
function stateMortgagePayment() payable {
        require(mortgagePayment.current_c_fact == C_facts.Requested );
        require(msg.value == amount_of_payment);
        acceptSub(mortgagePayment);
        amount_paid += msg.value;
        pendingWithdrawal += msg.value;

        if (amount_paid == amount) {
                state();
                mortgageCompletion.acceptPropertyPayingOff();
        } else {
                rejectMortgagePayment();
        }
}
```

We also contribute to the evolution of the notation in [11, 12] to illustrate model elements that will have to be implemented in the blockchain and again introduce a finer grained approach when using the CAD diagram and FDT table to clearly illustrate blockchain-related elements.

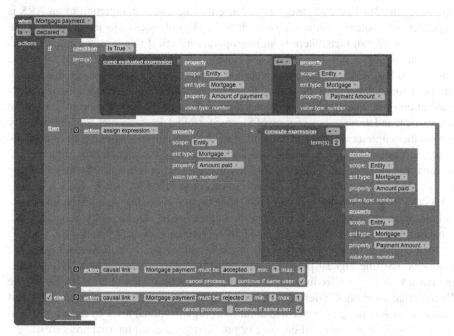

Fig. 10. Action rule for the declaration of the "Mortgage payment" transaction

when	mortgage payment for Mortgage is stated (T6/st) with the amount paid for Mortgage is some Money
assess	justice: the performer of the state is the payer for Mortgage sincerity: <no specific conditions > truth: with the amount paid for Mortgage is equal to the amount of each payment for Mortgage
if	complying with request is considered justifiable
then	accept mortgage payment for Mortgage [T6/ac]
else	reject mortgage payment for Mortgage [T6/rj]

Fig. 11. Action rule for the declaration of the "Mortgage payment" transaction in the previous ARS standard

Although a couple of smart contract related adornments were projected for the PM, its full range of implications are yet to be disclosed and will have to be left for future work. We consider that it will be very interesting to research the impact of combining different meta-elements from DEMO's essential models and understand how they could impact the blockchain, contract generation, interoperability, etc.

It is of particular interest to analyze the implications of assigning expressions (e.g. to update facts) when the ARs for a C-act are executed by the SC or the AR execution engine of an EIS. In either case, and because the successful completion of an ARS is dependent on contextual information such as the current process, its transactions or the attributes of known facts, there is an interoperability effort that must be studied. This effort encompasses, not only events and remote calls involving the EISs of interested parties and the SC itself, but also calls to the addresses of known oracles that satisfy the need for updated attribute data that is external to the contract and unknown at its generation-time. The relyance on oracles does not come without a compromise because the trustless and decentralized nature of SCs are forfeited due to oracles being technically yet another contract whose data is maintained by third parties. Other layers of possible ramifications can be added. For instance, when enclosed transactions are implemented as separate referenceable contracts, inside the enclosing contract or left outside of the BC altogether. Moreover, when taking into account DEMO's actors, roles and their respective functions and delegations, data sovereignty issues like data access and usage policies emerge. These issues, when in the context of an automatically generated SC, must be studied and tackled, for instance, by relying on the i4trust[2] platform.

Although the focus of this paper is at the border of the organization, where smart contracts have the highest potential to support business transactions involving multiple parties, and as per feedback obtained during the discussion at the 12th Enterprise Engineering Working Conference, BC and SCs also have the potential to re-shape and facilitate how auditing is performed at an intra-organizational level by monitoring and controlling the transactions of ongoing or previously executed internal processes.

There is also an opportunity to have a clearer understanding of the semantics associated with each composing piece, meaning action rule, of a contract. Although it is not

---
[2] https://i4trust.org/

within the scope of this paper, one might speculate about the reuse potential of our ARS and how it correlates with correctly produced and understood contracts. Ultimately, this approach may lead to non-experts to behave as a (very rough) approximation of a jurist. Moreover, and even if it is not in the sphere of competences for everyone to be an expert law-maker, the authors cannot help but wonder if this sort of contract generation is, at the very least, also adequate to produce actual legislation.

6 Conclusions

In this paper we propose a solution towards the automatic generation of smart contracts from DEMO models that, in our perspective, garners the best of the literature review and brings added value as a guide to future implementations of DEMO-based information systems. As there are a multitude of real world enterprise engineering problems that can be tackled with DEMO, we believe that it would be a capital mistake to not incorporate in its methodology the facilitating by-product of adopting a particular technology or implementation choice in the meta-models of extensions that can be easily curated and frequently revised by the community. These extensions do not compromise the formalism of the methodology and the EE theories but brings it closer to implementation. In this case, the adoption of smart contracts, entails a very advantageous technological approach to enterprise interoperability and (the client) demands new artifacts (tables, adornments, meta-elements, etc.) to understand and untap its full potential. Although the synergized potential of DEMO with smart contracts is evident by the body of work that has been published in recent years, it is the authors opinion that its true ramifications are yet to be discovered and will only be revealed, alongside the essence of organization, in actual business cases from the industry.

Acknowledgments. This work was supported by the program PROCiência 2020, funded by the European Regional Development Fund (ERDF), project MiColEC (M1420-01-0247-FEDER-000072).

References

1. Nakamoto, S.: Bitcoin: A Peer-to-Peer Electronic Cash System. Cryptogr. Mail. List https://www.metzdowd.com/mailman/listinfo/cryptography (2009)
2. Szabo, N.: Smart Contracts: Building Blocks for Digital Markets. https://www.fon.hum.uva.nl/rob/Courses/InformationInSpeech/CDROM/Literature/LOTwinterschool2006/szabo.best.vwh.net/smart_contracts_2.html
3. Aparício, M., et al.: Automated DEMO action model implementation using blockchain smart contracts. Apresentado na 12th International Conference on Knowledge Engineering and Ontology Development setembro 30 (2022)
4. Aparício, M., Guerreiro, S., Sousa, P.: Decentralized Enforcement of DEMO Action Rules Using Blockchain Smart Contracts. Apresentado na março 22 (2021)
5. Hornáčková, B., Skotnica, M., Pergl, R.: Exploring a role of blockchain smart contracts in enterprise engineering. In: Aveiro, D., Guizzardi, G., Guerreiro, S., Guédria, W. (eds.) EEWC 2018. LNBIP, vol. 334, pp. 113–127. Springer, Cham (2019). https://doi.org/10.1007/978-3-030-06097-8_7

6. Choudhury, O., Rudolph, N., Sylla, I., Fairoza, N., Das, A.: Auto-generation of smart contracts from domain-specific ontologies and semantic rules. In: 2018 IEEE International Conference on Internet of Things (iThings) and IEEE Green Computing and Communications (Green-Com) and IEEE Cyber, Physical and Social Computing (CPSCom) and IEEE Smart Data (SmartData), pp. 963–970 (2018)
7. Skotnica, M., Pergl, R.: Das Contract - a visual domain specific language for modeling blockchain smart contracts. In: Aveiro, D., Guizzardi, G., Borbinha, J. (eds.) EEWC 2019. LNBIP, vol. 374, pp. 149–166. Springer, Cham (2020). https://doi.org/10.1007/978-3-030-37933-9_10
8. Pacheco, D., Aveiro, D., Pinto, D., Gouveia, B.: Towards the x-theory: an evaluation of the perceived quality and functionality of DEMO's process model. In: Aveiro, D., Proper, H.A., Guerreiro, S., de Vries, M. (eds.) Advances in Enterprise Engineering XV, pp. 129–148. Springer, Cham (2022). https://doi.org/10.1007/978-3-031-11520-2_9
9. Pacheco, D., Aveiro, D., Gouveia, B., Pinto, D.: Evaluation of the perceived quality and functionality of fact model diagrams in DEMO. In: Aveiro, D., Proper, H.A., Guerreiro, S., de Vries, M. (eds.) Advances in Enterprise Engineering XV. pp. 114–128. Springer, Cham (2022). https://doi.org/10.1007/978-3-031-11520-2_8
10. 2020-07-31 DEMO Specification Language 4.5 – Enterprise Engineering Institute. https://ee-institute.org/mdocs-posts/2020-07-31-demo-specification-language-4-5/
11. Pinto, D., Aveiro, D., Pacheco, D., Gouveia, B., Gouveia, D.: Validation of DEMO's conciseness quality and proposal of improvements to the process model. In: Aveiro, D., Guizzardi, G., Pergl, R., Proper, H.A. (eds.) EEWC 2020. LNBIP, vol. 411, pp. 133–152. Springer, Cham (2021). https://doi.org/10.1007/978-3-030-74196-9_8
12. Gouveia, B., Aveiro, D., Pacheco, D., Pinto, D., Gouveia, D.: Fact model in DEMO - urban law case and proposal of representation improvements. In: Aveiro, D., Guizzardi, G., Pergl, R., Proper, H.A. (eds.) EEWC 2020. LNBIP, vol. 411, pp. 173–190. Springer, Cham (2021). https://doi.org/10.1007/978-3-030-74196-9_10
13. Dietz, J.L.G., Mulder, H.B.F.: The DEMO methodology. In: Dietz, J.L.G., Mulder, H.B.F. (eds.) Enterprise Ontology: A Human-Centric Approach to Understanding the Essence of Organisation, pp. 261–299. Springer, Cham (2020). https://doi.org/10.1007/978-3-030-38854-6_12
14. Dietz, J.L.G., Mulder, H.B.F.: The enterprise engineering theories. In: Dietz, J.L.G., Mulder, H.B.F. (eds.) Enterprise Ontology: A Human-Centric Approach to Understanding the Essence of Organisation, pp. 23–48. Springer, Cham (2020). https://doi.org/10.1007/978-3-030-38854-6_4
15. Dietz, J.: Enterprise Ontology: Theory and Methodology. Springer, New York (2006)
16. Andrade, M., Aveiro, D., Pinto, D.: Bridging ontology and implementation with a new DEMO action meta-model and engine. In: Aveiro, D., Guizzardi, G., Borbinha, J. (eds.) EEWC 2019. LNBIP, vol. 374, pp. 66–82. Springer, Cham (2020). https://doi.org/10.1007/978-3-030-37933-9_5
17. Pilkington, M.: Blockchain technology: principles and applications. Res. Handb. Digit. Transform, 225–253 (2016)
18. Solidity — Solidity 0.8.17 documentation. https://docs.soliditylang.org/en/v0.8.17/
19. Mavridou, A., Laszka, A.: Designing Secure Ethereum Smart Contracts: A Finite State Machine Based Approach (2017). http://arxiv.org/abs/1711.09327
20. Tallyn, E., Revans, J., Morgan, E., Fisken, K., Murray-Rust, D.: Enacting the last mile: experiences of smart contracts in courier deliveries. In: Proceedings of the 2021 CHI Conference on Human Factors in Computing Systems, pp. 1–14. Association for Computing Machinery, New York, NY, USA (2021)
21. Kim, H.M., Laskowski, M.: Toward an ontology-driven blockchain design for supply-chain provenance. Intell. Syst. Account. Finan. Manage. **25**(1), 18–27 (2018)

22. Iansiti, M., Lakhani, K.: The truth about blockchain. Harvard Bus. Rev. **95**, 118–127 (2017)
23. Francisco, K., Swanson, R.: The supply chain has no clothes: technology adoption of blockchain for supply chain transparency. Logistics **2**, 2 (2018). https://doi.org/10.3390/log istics2010002
24. Hevner, A.R., March, S.T., Park, J., Ram, S.: Design science in information systems research. MIS Q. **28**, 75–105 (2004). https://doi.org/10.2307/25148625
25. Hevner, A.R.: A three cycle view of design science research. Scand. J. Inf. Syst. **19**, 87–92 (2007)

Towards a FAIR-ready Data Value Chain for Dataspaces

Ben Hellmanzik[(✉)] and Kurt Sandkuhl

University of Rostock, Rostock, Germany
{ben.hellmanzik,kurt.sandkuhl}@uni-rostock.de

Abstract. Digital transformation has resulted in the availability of more data in higher quality and business models aiming at exploiting them, both on the level of individual enterprises and digital ecosystems. Among the essential elements of business models are the value offering made to target groups and the value creation required for this. Using the example of the maritime dataspace MARISPACE-X, the paper investigates an approach to support business model development combining data value chains with data sovereignty based on the FAIR principles as differentiating feature. The contributions of this paper are (1) an innovative dataspace as example case for business model development, (2) an approach to integrate FAIR principles into data value chains, and (3) analysis of existing literature in the field.

Keywords: Data value chain · FAIR · dataspace

1 Introduction

Digital transformation of many industrial areas has resulted in the availability of more data in often higher quality and business models aiming at exploiting them, both on the level of individual enterprises and digital ecosystems. Examples on enterprise-level are smart connected products, digital business services or product-service-systems. Examples on digital ecosystem level are quantified products and dataspace-based ecosystem (cf. Sect. 3.1). Among the essential elements of business models are the value offering made to target groups and the value creation required for this (cf. Section 3.3). When developing new business models, identification and analysis of these aspects are core challenges. For business models related to existing industry or domain developments, knowledge of these mechanisms can be an inspiration or even blueprint (see, e.g., Schallmo [40]). However, if such related areas do not exist or are not known, other approaches for identification and analysis are required. Using the example of the maritime dataspace MARISPACE-X (see Sect. 6, this paper investigates an approach to support business model development combining two dimensions:

- Data value chains and their different steps
- Data sovereignty based on the FAIR principles as differentiating feature of future business models

C. Griffo et al. (Eds.): EEWC 2022, LNBIP 473, pp. 90–105, 2023.
https://doi.org/10.1007/978-3-031-34175-5_6

The idea behind our approach is that data value chains most likely contain generic elements transferable to maritime dataspaces but implementation of FAIR principles requires services or techniques altering the established view of elements in data value chains. Combination of both is expected to create the nucleus for a future business model. The contributions of this paper are (1) an innovative dataspace as example case for business model development, (2) an approach to integrate FAIR principles into data value chains, and (3) analysis of existing literature in the field.

The paper is structured as follows: Sect. 2 introduces the research methodology used in the paper. Section 3 discusses relevant background from business models, dataspaces and the FAIR principles. Section 4 contains the results of the literature analysis. Section 5 proposes a FAIR-aware data value chain that is the result of enhancing an existing DVC approach identified in the literature analysis. In Sect. 6, the FAIR-aware data value chain is applied in the application example of a maritime dataspace. Section 7 summarizes the findings and gives an outlook to future work.

2   Research Methodology

This paper is part of a research project aiming at developing new business models for data-driven services in the context of dataspaces following the FAIR principles, and for implementing these business models in organizations, including the required adaptations of IT infrastructures, organisational structures and processes. The project follows the paradigm of design science research (DSR) [22] and this paper concerns the requirements analysis and first steps towards designing the envisioned artefact, a business model prototype and methodical/technical support for implementing it in organizations. More concrete, we focus in this paper on the value creation aspect of business models by analysing the data value chain. The research question for this paper is: **What adaptations in a data value chain are required for the support of FAIR principles?** The research approach used is a combination of literature study, argumentative-deductive work and descriptive case study. Starting from the research question, the literature study is used to identify established approaches for data value chains (DVC) and potential ways to tackle FAIR adaptation. As the literature study does not return any work on DVC-adaptations for FAIR, the next step is to analyse all DVC steps for required changes, which constitutes the argumentative-deductive part. Finally, the resulting DVC adapted for FAIR is subject to an initial validation by applying it in a use case. The motivation for the use case is that we need to explore the nature and phenomenon of FAIR-aware DVC in real-world environments, which is possible in case studies.

3   Background

3.1   Dataspaces

Dataspaces or, more precisely, platforms for managing dataspaces address the challenge of low-level data management across heterogeneous collections by dealing consistently and efficiently with large amounts of interrelated but disparately managed data. They provide mechanisms to identify sources in a dataspace and inter-relate them, offer basic query mechanisms over them, support for introspection, some mechanisms for enforcing constraints, and limited consistency and recovery.

There are several differences of dataspaces from traditional databases and data integration systems [18]: (1) Dataspaces must deal with data and services using these data in a wide variety of formats accessible through many systems with different interfaces. (2) Although a dataspace offers integrated means of managing data in the space, often the same data may also be accessible and modifiable through an interface native to the system hosting the data. (3) Queries to a dataspace may offer varying levels of completeness and accuracy, i.e., in some cases queries may return best-effort or approximate results at the time of the query. (4) Dataspace ares supposed to support tighter integration of data in the space as necessary by offering tools and pathways.

Recent research on dataspaces included technological aspects of dataspace management and the perspective of ecosystems related to dataspaces. The GAIA-X project provides technical specifications for deploying security-enforcing cooperation and communication infrastructures [5]. The International Data Spaces (IDS) ecosystem recommends business roles and application development guidelines for companies willing to join an IDS ecosystem [21]. The intended result is a trusted environment for industries to share operational data to support core capabilities [35]. GAIA-X and IDS are two major initiatives for forming the European IDS vision.

3.2   FAIR Principles

The FAIR Principles are relatively new guidelines that were originally intended to serve primarily the scientific community and were first published in the journal "Scientific Data" in 2016 [47]. The origin of the FAIR principles lies in the fact that academics have been concerned with the underlying digital ecosystem used to produce academic publications. The data produced here often cannot be exploited to the maximum, as data is rarely well managed and there was generally no clarity about what constitutes good data management. This situation should be addressed and solved with the FAIR principles. One concern of the FAIR principles is therefore the improvement of knowledge generation through human, but also computer-based interaction. The FAIR principles themselves include the four tasks of making data **F**indable, **A**ccessible, **I**nteroperable, and **R**eusable (Fig. 1).

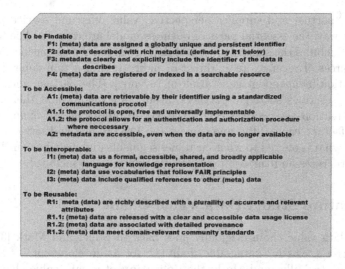

Fig. 1. The FAIR principles by Wilkinson et al. [47]

Especially in the maritime domain, FAIR principles can improve the current data management, as argued by Tanhua et al. [44]. The volume of maritime data has increased greatly recently. However, at the same time, these data are diverse, while additional complexity is created by new sensor formats. Best practices for data management are not well defined, and data management structures vary widely. It is for this use case that the standardization of data and the application of FAIR principles can be beneficial, according to Tanhua et al. [44]. This leads to a more open ecosystem where not only closely related researchers can share data, but also stakeholders outside the research community.

3.3 Business Models

Business models have been an important element of economic behavior for many years and received significantly growing attention in research with the beginning of the Internet economy. In general, the business model of an enterprise describes the essential elements that create and deliver a value proposition for the customers, including the economic model and underlying logic, the key assets and core competences [34]. Zott and Amit identified three major fields of research in business model developments [53]: (1) business models for electronic business contexts and the use of IT in organizations, (2) strategic business models for competitive advantage, value creation and organizational performance, and (3) business models in innovation and technology management. The first two fields are considered relevant for our research as they affect value creation processes and positioning in the market. Analysis and design of business models can be supported by approaches dividing business models into several perspectives. Partial business models, as defined by Wirtz [48] or business model dimensions proposed by Schallmo [40] can support these tasks. The perspectives covered in both approaches are: financial perspective, customer perspective, value creation perspective, partner and supplier perspective, value offer and service perspective. In this way, the essential parts of business model are covered. The financial perspective includes the sources of capital that are necessary for business activity and the sources of revenues (e.g., direct or indirect; transaction-dependent and the transaction-independent generation of revenue). The partner and supplier perspective describes strategic partners, production factors and their sources. The value creation perspectives covers the way of producing goods and services with input factors, capabilities and core assets. The product and service perspective defines what is offered to what customer segments and distribution channels. Demand structures and the competitive situation are also included.

4   Literature Study: Data Value Chain

The term data value chain originally goes back to Miller and Mork [31], who refer to Porter's "classic" data value chain [37] for its development.

According to Miller and Mork, the **definition** of a data value chain is: "A series of activities, that create and build value, through: (1) Management and coordination across the service continuum from data generators to information consumers seeking to make decisions. (2) Forming a collaborative partnership and Coordinating data collections from various stakeholders. (3) Analyzing Data to optimize service delivery and quality decisions. (4) Streamlining data management activities to enable positive outcomes for all relevant stakeholders. (5) Establishing a portfolio management approach to invest in people, processes, and technology that maximize the value of the combined data and inform decisions that enhance the organizations performance."

The search for suitable literature reviews, using the terms "literature review", and the synonyms "literature analysis", "systematic review" and "structured review" in conjunction with "data value chains" did not yield any results. Therefore, it is appropriate to conduct a literature search. In order to understand how the concept of the data value chain has developed from Miller and Morks perspective and whether there may be starting points that enable an adaptation to the FAIR principles, a literature search according to Kitchenham [26] is carried out below. The databases used for the scoping review were: Scopus, IEEExplore and Web of Science. The final search string used in this research was "Data Value Chain". A combination with "Maritime" and "Fair" in the string did not reveal any deeper understanding of the topic. This resulted in a set of 122 documents that were classified according to the following inclusion and exclusion criteria. **Inclusion criteria**: Explicit definitions of data value chains, graphical illustrations, reference to the maritime domain or economic applicability, consecutive steps of a data value chain. **Exclusion criteria**: Lack of relevance due to lack of definitions or explicit Data Value Chains, publications where the term 'data value chain' was only found in the abstract or where data value chains were used in a very narrow context. Through this approach, 80 documents were identified that are at least weakly relevant to answering the question of how data value chains have developed and what economic evaluations they can have on business models. Of these 80 documents, 39 are clearly suitable for mapping a data value chain. Based on these 39 documents, an attempt is made to outline the contents of a data value chain for the maritime sector as a basis for applying the FAIR principles in this area. The procedure for identifying the relevant literature can be traced by the diagram in Fig. 2. The following tables should give an overview of the focal points of the papers found. It should be noted that many literature examples have a rather general interest in the processing of Big Data and are not related to any specific domain. This is covered by the topics "General" and "Big Data Processing" (Table 1).

Table 1. Focal Points and Sources regarding Data Value Chains

Focal Points	Sources
Big Data Processing	[17, 19, 20, 30, 33, 38, 39, 49, 50]
Big Data Quality	[1, 9, 11, 15, 41]
Data Value Chain (Management)	[3, 6, 8, 10, 23, 25, 31]
Value Creation/Monetisation	[4, 13, 14, 16, 29]
Linked/Open Data	[28, 52]
Multimodal Data Value Chain	[42, 43]
Governance	[27, 51]
FAIR Data	[44]
Others	[2, 7, 12, 32, 45, 46, 54]

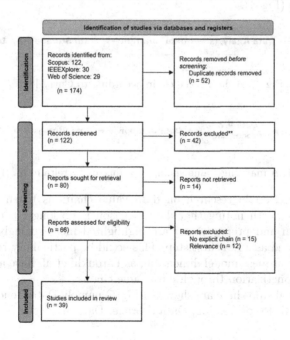

Fig. 2. Flow Diagram of the systematic literature review, inspired by [36]

The results of the literature review show that Data Value Chains are used in very different application domains. Furthermore, it can be seen that especially data quality, the processing of "Big Data", and value creation, are things to account for, if one wants to consider Data Value Chains.

Of particular interest are the following: The origins of the data value chain, data value chains for economic exploitation (as a link to value creation in business models) and the application of data value chains in the maritime domain.

Since the article by Miller and Mork refers in particular to the foundations of Porter, which in turn is one of the foundations for the business models of Wirtz [48] or Schallmo [40], the phases in this approach should be briefly examined. The Data Value Chain according to Mork and Miller comprises the steps Data Discovery, with the sub-steps Collect and Annotate, Prepare and Organise, Data Integration, and Data Exploitation with the sub-steps Analyze, Visualize and Make Decisions. In fact, approaches that reflect the FAIR principles can be found here, for example through the Collect and Annotate step. The Prepare step can also cover some of the requirements that make data "accessible". In Miller and Mork's overview, however, the data storage and preprocessing steps are missing, and the decision making step is only one of the options available with the underlying and processed data. The application of data value chains in the maritime domain (e.g. Lytra [30] and Ferreira [17]) point to the adaption of Curry's [8] Data Value Chain which can be seen in Fig. 3. The maritime data value chain presented by Ferreira et al. [17] is based on that data value chain, but at the same time adds stakeholders and activities in the individual steps, as well as preprocessing and the measurement step, which is merged with the data acquisition step (Fig. 4).

Fig. 3. A data value chain according to Curry [8]

Fig. 4. A maritime value chain according to Ferreira et al. [17]

Another direction in research on data value chains is taken by Faroukhi et al. [14]. It is worth noting that data curation is no longer a priority here, but visualisation and preprocessing are highlighted more strongly, while data generation is listed as a new first step. This could be particularly relevant when considering the business model dimension, as Faroukhi et al. have also looked in particular at monetization through data value chains.

The individual steps here are shown in Fig. 5, namely Data Generation, Data Acquisition, Data Preprocessing, Data Storage, Data Analysis, Data Visualisation and Data Exposition.

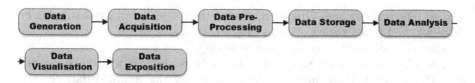

Fig. 5. Data Value Chain according to Faroukhi et al. [14]

In the context of this work, it seems to makes sense to keep the step of data curation because it contains explicit steps of FAIRification of data sets. It is also suited for the maritime domain, as the literature review shows. At the same time, the steps that Curry has taken to map the individual steps of a data value chain do not seem to be sufficient enough, as preprocessing in particular often appears explicitly in other data value chains (e.g. [13,17,24].

The following table shows, which FAIR principles are explicitly mentioned in Curry's Data Value Chain and what Value Creation can be derived from the FAIR principles (Table 2).

Table 2. FAIR principle, Value Creation and Mapping on Curry's DVC

FAIR principle	Value Creation included	Mapping on Curry's DVC Steps
Findable	URI, easy access to data and meta-data, searchable for users	Not explicitly stated could be included in Data Usage
Accessible	Authentication and Authorisation Protocols for secure handling of the data used	Not explicitly stated
Interoperable	Data can be used accross different enterprise parts and even different enterprises	Explicitly stated in the Curation Step
Reusable	Data Value remains more steady over time, Dependencies from Domain Experts can be reduced	Not explicitly stated, but a possible result of Data Curation

As can be seen from this tabular overview, the FAIR principles are dealt with rather indirectly in Data Value Chains. Therefore, we propose to include explicit steps in Data Value Chains to take the FAIR principles into account.

5 FAIR Adaption for Data Value Chains

Since it has already become apparent that Curry's "data curation" step may have been defined too broadly, we propose to integrate finer steps into the data value chain. For this we will use the Data Value Chain by Kaiser et al. [23] as a basis: The authors have already presented their work in an explicit industry (Vehicles) and based their work on Curry's Data Value Chain.

The steps and definitions here are as follows:

Data Generation describes how data can be recorded in a direct or indirect way. **Data Acquisition** includes the collection of the recorded data, or the ability to access the recorded data. **Pre-processing** includes, in particular, the cleaning of data records, anonymisation and, if necessary, standardisation or normalisation. The **Data analysis** serves in particular the purpose of being able to draw information from the existing data. This can include statistical methods such as outlier detection, machine learning methods, but also simple or advanced visualisations. **Data Storage** is, according to Curry "the persistence and management of data in a scalable way that satisfies the needs of applications that require fast access to the data" [8] **Data Usage** describes the use of the underlying data. This can include buying and selling the raw data, as well as the use for economic purposes and the use of the respective intermediate results of the data value chain as input for applications, for example.It should be noted that the visualisation step in our Data Value Chain falls within the analysis step: extracting information can be done by visualising the results of statistical procedures, so visualisation is not a separate step (Fig. 6).

Fig. 6. The basis of our data value chain, adopted from Kaiser et al. [23]

We propose to explicitly include the generation of metadata in the data value chain. The step of **meta data generation** therefore includes the inclusion of the "technical" parameters in data acquisition, such as time, source, coordinates, data provider, sensor format, resolution, contact person, organisation, etc. In addition, the **assessment/qualification** step is to be introduced. This serves to determine whether a data set is at all suitable for the planned use and, if necessary, to establish suitability. For example, missing (meta) data can be added and quality metrics can be included in the data set.The **indexing/registering** step serves to make the data findable, for example by entering meta data in appropriate directories and using global identifiers. The **licensing and sovereignty** step could in principle be part of data usage, but is made explicit here: the rights of use and exploitation of the data should be clarified in this step and at best made available as metadata.

The changes are visible in the following figure (Fig. 7):

By introducing these individual, explicit steps, the FAIR principles can be applied in Data Value Chains. This should lead to increased quality of the data used and also create interoperability across a domain.

This approach is currently only theoretical, but will be discussed with partners from the maritime domain within the Marispace-X project and adapted if

Fig. 7. Changes made to the Data Value Chain to make it FAIR-ready

necessary. The results so far suggest that FAIRification of datasets deserve special attention as they can solve domain-specific problems of maritime use cases. Clarifying the individual steps can help to better estimate workloads, generate meaningful metadata, improve collaboration between project partners and potentially open up new application areas. The use of a Data Value Chain with FAIR principles is one of the starting points of these goals and can be used as the core of digital business models in the maritime domain.

The benefits of the Data Value Chain in practical application can be seen by applying a Value Chain/Business Model Element Matrix (for example with values such as value creation, actors involved, potential impact for customers etc.) for the maritime domain. In this way, the benefits of the individual steps for a business model can be analysed and possible potentials identified.

6 Use Case: Maritime Dataspace MARISPACE-X

For an initial evaluation of the FAIR-ready DVC, this section uses the case of an ecosystem related to the maritime dataspace MARISPACE-X. Starting from a brief introduction of the use case in Sect. 6.1, Sect. 6.2 discusses the DVC in MARISPACE-X, the need for applying FAIR principles and the suitability of the FAIR-ready DVC.

6.1 Case Description

The MARISPACE-X project aims at developing a cross-domain maritime ecosystem of data and federated services. Its partners include large-scale dataspace infrastructure providers, scientific and public organisations offering maritime sensor data, service providers in the field of data processing and application partners. The project aims to develop scalable, federated and sovereign services for data management and information extraction and presentation by combining edge and Fog computing with centralized cloud-based management.

Among the application cases considered in the project is the case of Offshore Wind Farms: During the life cycle of an offshore wind farm, immense amounts of data are generated by the turbines themselves, but also by project planning and asset monitoring. Intelligent management and analysis of data in the context of Federated Services has to support the overall lifecycle of the wind farm, from the planning phase through to decommissioning. In this context, the services and collaboration options developed within MARISPACE-X enable a significant increase in performance, the optimization of asset handling as well as the possibility of efficient multiple use of data. As this has a concrete impact on the competitiveness of the offshore wind farm operators, the targeted cost reduction can have a direct impact on the EEG (Law for renewable energies in Germany) surcharge financed by the taxpayer and thus on electricity prices. The targeted digitalization leap will also lead to more efficient processes and thus also contributes to accelerating the energy transition.

6.2   FAIR DVC in MARISPACE-X

In MARISPACE-X, definition of data-driven services and business models linked to these services is still in progress, i.e. the DVC in MARISPACE-X is not yet explicitly defined. However, the different project partners in MARISPACE-X represent typical roles in an ecosystem and the current business activities and service offerings can be mapped to the steps in Kaiser's extension of Curry's DVC approach:

- maritime sensor data providers: take care of data generation and part of the data acquisition. Data generation, for example, can be performed with underwater vehicles scanning the sea ground for geological information required in planning offshore wind parks.
- dataspace infrastructure providers: provide data storage accessible for sensor data providers, pre-processing service providers and application partners, for example by using the GAIA-X platform.
- data processing service providers: pre-process the sensor data (e.g. by filtering and transforming) for different groups of application partners
- application partners: apply the sensor data, for example for planning and designing offshore wind parks. This usually also includes data analysis steps, e.g., for determining the suitability of geological formations for grounding underwater anchors for wind parks.

The above confirms that MARISPACE-X is an application case for DVCs.

Next, we need to confirm the necessity for FAIR principles in the application domain: In the maritime domain, the preservation of data sovereignty (data protection, interoperability, modularity) in the processing and processing and analysis of sensor data across all levels (edge/ fog/ cloud) are of particular importance. The reason for this is the interaction of various players in the process of data acquisition, data management and data analysis as well as the resulting complex procedures. The maritime sector is particularly suitable, as data collection is many times more complex and heterogeneous than on land, and the technological developments, especially in the field of autonomous underwater and surface vehicles, as well as the intensification of the use of the oceans will lead to an exponential increase in data in the short term.

As a final step of this initial evaluation, the suitability of the FAIR DVC has to be investigated. The main difference of the FAIR DVC compared to the conventional DVC are additional value chain steps. All additional steps are visible and required in MARISPACE-X:

- meta data generation: is required to capture, for example, origin, ownership and intellectual property rights of the sensor data providers and attach them in a suitable format to the original data.
- assessment/qualification: is a precondition for application partners and pre-processing service providers to decide, what sensor data is applicable in what application-specific processing step
- indexing/registering: is required to make sensor data findable in the infrastructure and dataspace
- licensing and sovereignty: is essential to allow for value exchange, participation and business models in the ecosystem

7   Summary and Future Work

Starting from a literature analysis in the field of DVC, we investigated the suitability of contemporary DVC models for FAIR principles, analysed missing steps, and proposed an extension accommodating missing value creation steps. This extension, the FAIR-ready DVC, was applied in the ecosystem related to the maritime dataspace MARISPACE-X to show its applicability. The biggest limitation of our existing work is the application in only one use case so far. More work on refining the FAIR-ready DVC, application in other application domains and refinement in more detailed use cases is required. The need for a data value chain or a similar construct also appears in the context of FAIRification of data in the maritime domain. The aim of the MARISPACE-X project, however, is to also enable the economic utilisation of maritime data.

References

1. Alaoui, I.E., Gahi, Y.: The impact of big data quality on sentiment analysis approaches. Procedia Comput. Sci. **160**, 803–810 (2019)
2. Attard, J., Brennan, R.: DaVe: a semantic data value vocabulary to enable data value characterisation. In: Hammoudi, S., Śmiałek, M., Camp, O., Filipe, J. (eds.) ICEIS 2018. LNBIP, vol. 363, pp. 239–261. Springer, Cham (2019). https://doi.org/10.1007/978-3-030-26169-6_12
3. Attard, J., Orlandi, F., Auer, S.: Exploiting the value of data through data value networks. In: Baguma, R., De', R., Janowski, T. (eds.) Proceedings of the 10th International Conference on Theory and Practice of Electronic Governance, pp. 475–484. ACM, New York (2017)
4. Badewitz, W., Kloker, S., Weinhardt, C.: The data provision game: researching revenue sharing in collaborative data networks, vol 1, pp. 191–200 (2020). https://www.scopus.com/inward/record.uri?eid=2-s2.0-85089283575&doi=10.1109%2fCBI49978.2020.00028&partnerID=40&md5=8f2e77fad3c0db43a6204249b44558b2
5. Braud, A., Fromentoux, G., Radier, B., Le Grand, O.: The road to European digital sovereignty with gaia-x and idsa. IEEE Netw. **35**(2), 4–5 (2021)

6. Brennan, R., Attard, J., Helfert, M.: Management of data value chains, a value monitoring capability maturity model, vol. 2, pp. 573–584 (2018). https://www.scopus.com/inward/record.uri?eid=2-s2.0-85047758633&doi=10.5220%2f0006684805730584&partnerID=40&md5=0383f6ee5eda49ea8aecec5686e19ee1

7. Correndo, G., Crowle, S., Papay, J., Boniface, M.: Enhancing marine industry risk management through semantic reconciliation of underwater iot data streams, pp. 161–168 (2016)

8. Curry, E.: The big data value chain: definitions, concepts, and theoretical approaches. In: Cavanillas, J.M., Curry, E., Wahlster, W. (eds.) New Horizons for a Data-Driven Economy, pp. 29–37. Springer, Cham (2016). https://doi.org/10.1007/978-3-319-21569-3_3

9. El Alaoui, I., Gahi, Y., Messoussi, R.: Big data quality metrics for sentiment analysis approaches. In: Proceedings of the 2019 International Conference on Big Data Engineering, pp. 36–43. ACM, New York (2019)

10. El Kadiri, S., et al.: Current trends on ICT technologies for enterprise information systems. Comput. Ind. **79**, 14–33 (2016)

11. Elouataoui, W., Alaoui, I.E., Gahi, Y.: Data quality in the era of big data: a global review. In: Baddi, Y., Gahi, Y., Maleh, Y., Alazab, M., Tawalbeh, L. (eds.) Big Data Intelligence for Smart Applications. SCI, vol. 994, pp. 1–25. Springer, Cham (2022). https://doi.org/10.1007/978-3-030-87954-9_1

12. Emmanouilidis, C., et al.: Enabling the human in the loop: Linked data and knowledge in industrial cyber-physical systems. Ann. Rev. Control **47**, 249–265 (2019)

13. Faroukhi, A.Z., El Alaoui, I., Gahi, Y., Amine, A.: An adaptable big data value chain framework for end-to-end big data monetization. Big Data Cogn. Comput. **4**(4), 34 (2020)

14. Faroukhi, A.Z., El Alaoui, I., Gahi, Y., Amine, A.: Big data monetization throughout big data value chain: a comprehensive review. J. Big Data **7**(1), 1–22 (2020)

15. Faroukhi, A.Z., El Alaoui, I., Gahi, Y., Amine, A.: Big data value chain: a unified approach for integrated data quality and security (2020). https://www.scopus.com/inward/record.uri?eid=2-s2.0-85100075838&doi=10.1109%2fICECOCS50124.2020.9314391&partnerID=40&md5=981b16ae83fceed969b3b106a3862d70

16. Faroukhi, A.Z., El Alaoui, I., Gahi, Y., Amine, A.: A novel approach for big data monetization as a service. In: Saeed, F., Al-Hadhrami, T., Mohammed, F., Mohammed, E. (eds.) Advances on Smart and Soft Computing. AISC, vol. 1188, pp. 153–165. Springer, Singapore (2021). https://doi.org/10.1007/978-981-15-6048-4_14

17. Ferreira, J., et al.: Maritime data technology landscape and value chain exploiting oceans of data for maritime applications, vol. 2018-January, pp. 1113–1122 (2018). https://www.scopus.com/inward/record.uri?eid=2-s2.0-85047546255&doi=10.1109%2fICE.2017.8280006&partnerID=40&md5=32c3768be5303cd8654586e2f1e2e608

18. Halevy, A., Franklin, M., Maier, D.: Principles of dataspace systems. In: Proceedings of the Twenty-Fifth ACM SIGMOD-SIGACT-SIGART Symposium on Principles of Database Systems, pp. 1–9 (2006)

19. Hu, H., Wen, Y., Chua, T.S., Li, X.: Toward scalable systems for big data analytics: a technology tutorial. IEEE Access **2**, 652–687 (2014)

20. Imasheva, B., Nakispekov, A., Sidelkovskaya, A., Sidelkovskiy, A.: The practice of moving to big data on the case of the nosql database, clickhouse. In: Advances in Intelligent Systems and Computing, vol. 991, pp. 820–828 (2020). https://www. scopus.com/inward/record.uri?eid=2-s2.0-85068388124&doi=10.1007%2f978-3-030-21803-4_82&partnerID=40&md5=7ad418e532ac391bcb06014b0231b508
21. International Data Spaces Association: Idsa rule book version 1.0: White paper of the ids association. https://internationaldataspaces.org/wp-content/uploads/dlm_uploads/IDSA-White-Paper-IDSA-Rule-Book.pdf
22. Johannesson, P., Perjons, E.: An Introduction to Design Science, vol. 10. Springer, Heidelberg (2014). https://doi.org/10.1007/978-3-319-10632-8
23. Kaiser, C., Festl, A., Pucher, G., Fellmann, M., Stocker, A.: The vehicle data value chain as a lightweight model to describe digital vehicle services. In: Proceedings of the 15th International Conference on Web Information Systems and Technologies, pp. 68–79. SCITEPRESS - Science and Technology Publications (2019)
24. Kaiser, C., Festl, A., Pucher, G., Fellmann, M., Stocker, A.: Digital services based on vehicle usage data: the underlying vehicle data value chain. In: Bozzon, A., Domínguez Mayo, F.J., Filipe, J. (eds.) WEBIST 2019. LNBIP, vol. 399, pp. 22–43. Springer, Cham (2020). https://doi.org/10.1007/978-3-030-61750-9_2
25. Kasim, H., Hung, T., Li, X.: Data value chain as a service framework: For enabling data handling, data security and data analysis in the cloud, pp. 804–809 (2012). https://www.scopus.com/inward/record.uri?eid=2-s2.0-84874063281&doi=10.1109%2fICPADS.2012.131&partnerID=40&md5=6f8915641ddf4206813823436b008529
26. Kitchenham, B.A., Charters, S.: Guidelines for performing systematic literature reviews in software engineering (2012)
27. König, P.D.: Citizen-centered data governance in the smart city: from ethics to accountability. Sustain. Cities Soc. **75**, 103308 (2021)
28. Latif, A., Scherp, A., Tochtermann, K.: Lod for library science: benefits of applying linked open data in the digital library setting. KI - Künstliche Intelligenz **30**(2), 149–157 (2016)
29. Lim, C., Kim, K.H., Kim, M.J., Heo, J.Y., Kim, K.J., Maglio, P.P.: From data to value: a nine-factor framework for data-based value creation in information-intensive services. Int. J. Inf. Manag. **39**, 121–135 (2018)
30. Lytra, I., Vidal, M.E., Orlandi, F., Attard, J.: A big data architecture for managing oceans of data and maritime applications. In: 2017 International Conference on Engineering, Technology and Innovation (ICE/ITMC), pp. 1216–1226 (2017)
31. Miller, H.G., Mork, P.: From data to decisions: a value chain for big data. IT Prof. **15**(1), 57–59 (2013)
32. Mörth, O., Emmanouilidis, C., Hafner, N., Schadler, M.: Cyber-physical systems for performance monitoring in production intralogistics. Comput. Ind. Eng. **142**, 106333 (2020)
33. Osman, A.M.S.: A novel big data analytics framework for smart cities. Future Gener. Comput. Syst. **91**, 620–633 (2019)
34. Osterwalder, A., Pigneur, Y.: Business Model Generation: A Handbook for Visionaries, Game Changers, and Challengers, vol. 1. John Wiley & Sons, Hoboken (2010)
35. Otto, B., Hompel, M., Wrobel, S.: International data spaces. In: Neugebauer, R. (ed.) Digital Transformation, pp. 109–128. Springer, Heidelberg (2019). https://doi.org/10.1007/978-3-662-58134-6_8
36. Page, M.J., et al.: Prisma 2020 explanation and elaboration: updated guidance and exemplars for reporting systematic reviews. BMJ 372 (2021). https://www.bmj.com/content/372/bmj.n160

37. Porter, M.E.: Competetive Advantage. The Free Press, New York (1985)
38. Ramannavar, M., Sidnal, N.S.: Big data and analytics—a journey through basic concepts to research issues. In: Suresh, L.P., Panigrahi, B.K. (eds.) Proceedings of the International Conference on Soft Computing Systems. AISC, vol. 398, pp. 291–306. Springer, New Delhi (2016). https://doi.org/10.1007/978-81-322-2674-1_29
39. Saeed, F., Al-Hadhrami, T., Mohammed, E., Mohammed, F. (eds.): Advances on smart and soft computing: Proceedings of ICACIn 2020, Advances in Intelligent Systems and Computing, vol. 1188. Springer, Singapore (2021). https://doi.org/10.1007/978-981-15-6048-4
40. Schallmo, D., Williams, C.A., Boardman, L.: Digital transformation of business models–best practice, enablers, and roadmap. In: Digital Disruptive Innovation, pp. 119–138. World Scientific (2020)
41. Serhani, M.A., El Kassabi, H.T., Taleb, I., Nujum, A.: An hybrid approach to quality evaluation across big data value chain. In: 2016 IEEE International Congress on Big Data (BigData Congress), pp. 418–425. IEEE (2016)
42. Shankar, S.K., Prieto, L.P., Rodriguez-Triana, M.J., Ruiz-Calleja, A.: A review of multimodal learning analytics architectures. In: 2018 IEEE 18th International Conference on Advanced Learning Technologies (ICALT), pp. 212–214. IEEE (2018)
43. Shankar, S.K., Rodriguez-Triana, M.J., Ruiz-Calleja, A., Prieto, L.P., Chejara, P., Martinez-Mones, A.: Multimodal data value chain (m-dvc): a conceptual tool to support the development of multimodal learning analytics solutions. IEEE Revista Iberoamericana de Tecnologias del Aprendizaje 15(2), 113–122 (2020)
44. Tanhua, T., et al.: Ocean fair data services. Front. Marine Sci. 6, 92 (2019)
45. Teisserenc, B., Sepasgozar, S.: Project data categorization, adoption factors, and non-functional requirements for blockchain based digital twins in the construction industry 4.0. Buildings 11(12), 626 (2021)
46. Victor, V., Maria, F.F.: Prospects of big data driven innovation in enterprises, pp. 4503–4510 (2018). https://www.scopus.com/inward/record.uri?eid=2-s2.0-85060824118&partnerID=40&md5=f405662d4278a278c3aaf087c8536aad
47. Wilkinson, M.D., et al.: The fair guiding principles for scientific data management and stewardship. Sci. Data 3, 160018 (2016)
48. Wirtz, B.W., Pistoia, A., Ullrich, S., Göttel, V.: Business models: origin, development and future research perspectives. Long Range Plan. 49(1), 36–54 (2016)
49. Wu, J.: Research on the transformation and upgrading path of traditional industries driven by big data from the perspective of big data value chain, vol. 1992 (2021). https://www.scopus.com/inward/record.uri?eid=2-s2.0-85114200500&doi=10.1088%2f1742-6596%2f1992%2f2%2f022175&partnerID=40&md5=a93a4e8d51d707b46758bf3da992e248
50. Yousfi, S., Chiadmi, D., Rhanoui, M.: Smart big data framework for insight discovery. J. King Saud Univ. Comput. Inf. Sci. 34, 9777–9792 (2022)
51. Yu, H., Foster, J.: Towards information governance of data value chains: balancing the value and risks of data within a financial services company. In: Uden, L., Lu, W., Ting, I.-H. (eds.) KMO 2017. CCIS, vol. 731, pp. 336–346. Springer, Cham (2017). https://doi.org/10.1007/978-3-319-62698-7_28
52. Zeleti, F.A., Ojo, A.: Open data value capability architecture. Inf. Syst. Front. 19(2), 337–360 (2017)

53. Zott, C., Amit, R.: Business model design: an activity system perspective. Long Range Plan. **43**(2–3), 216–226 (2010)
54. Åkerman, M., et al.: Challenges building a data value chain to enable data-driven decisions: a predictive maintenance case in 5g-enabled manufacturing, vol. 17, p. 411–418 (2018)

The Effect of Nudges, Visual Literacy and Their Interaction on Enhancing the Understanding of Enterprise Process Models

Iris Mulder$^{(\boxtimes)}$ and Mark A. T. Mulder

TEEC2, Hoevelaken, The Netherlands
iris23mulder@gmail.com, markmulder@teec2.nl

Abstract. In Enterprise Engineering (EE), like other fields, visual information has several advantages over text and we are used to represent a process model as visual information. However, little is known about the contributing factors that influence the understanding of these process models. Visual literacy and nudges are two potential contributing factors to the ability to understand process models and reduce clutter. In this study, we researched by using an online questionnaire ($N = 37$) whether we could enhance the understanding of process models with the help of nudges, visual literacy and the interaction effects between the nudges and visual literacy. We executed a univariate ANOVA to compare the effect of the nudges on the understanding of process models with the two nudge conditions, visual literacy and all possible interactions as predictors. The results showed that nudges do not significantly influence the understanding of process models, which was not in line with our expectations. Visual literacy may have a significant influence, which aligns with our expectations. There was one significant interaction between visual literacy and the arrow nudge; however, not in the direction that we expected, therefore, not in line with our expectations. Given our small sample size, our significance could rest on a coincidence. We offer no open-and-shut conclusions about enhancing the understanding of process models with the help of nudges, visual literacy and the interaction effects between the nudges and visual literacy.

Keywords: DEMO · enterprise engineering · visualisation · visual literacy · process model · interaction · nudges · social psychology · psychology

1 Introduction

In the EE field, we try to design and communicate our beliefs of a better organisation using models. This communication is inspired by the scientific designed drawings with a clear semantic that is derived from the studied literature. In Design and Engineering Methodology for Organisations (DEMO) we have a transaction kind that is represented as a contraction of the product and the

C. Griffo et al. (Eds.): EEWC 2022, LNBIP 473, pp. 106–120, 2023.
https://doi.org/10.1007/978-3-031-34175-5_7

communication, represented by a diamond and circle, respectively. We use the transaction kind to communicate, among other things, the essential process of the organisation. Recent studies have stated that this process representation not always fulfils all goals of communicating the desired information [19,22].

Visual language has existed 25,000 years longer than written language [17]. Visual information has several advantages over text: visuals require less effort to recognise, are easier to recall [8] and are more powerful in expressing abstract knowledge [25]. Additionally, "Visual displays provide the highest bandwidth channel from the computer to the human." as Ware put it [28]. One way to visualise abstract knowledge is by the use of process models. However, little is known about the contributing factors that influence the understanding of these process models [23]. It is an aspiration for the designer that process models are intuitive and easy to digest for people with different levels of knowledge and expertise; however, current practice shows that this is a challenging goal. Navigating the potential decisions to optimise a visualisation is complex and lacks sufficient research and knowledge at this time [2]. Currently, there is little information available about which representation methods for visualisations are effective or efficient [16]. Additionally, which visual attributes are most helpful in conveying specific information is unclear. Applying specific visual dimensions within a visualisation is one of the essential factors for its comprehension. In this thesis, we will investigate if specific visual information, a nudge, will help the understanding of process models.

Visualisations are representations of complex information constructed in such a way that it is supposed to enhance understanding [2]. Visualising data is essential to scientific practice to communicate crucial information to others in an understandable format. However, in companies where visualisations are used to convey essential information through process models, improvement is needed to achieve understanding within different levels of an organisation. According to Mulder [19] comprehension of process models, in practice, is experienced as more of a problem on the employment level of C-level executives. A C-level executive (e.g. CEO, CFO, CTO) is a person who holds a senior position, plays a strategic role within the organisation, and impacts company-wide decisions. Visualisations are currently used to enable communication of information that is difficult to convey or too cumbersome to convey in words [2]. One way to support understanding visualisations is using short textual captions. A short textual caption is an example of signalling. Signalling refers to using textual information to direct the attention within a visualisation to support the cognitive process of comprehension [2]. That means that this information is inherently integrated with visualisations to provide context. Therefore, it is also essential to optimise coherence between the visualisation and the supporting text in ways that aid understanding.

So far, research points out that experts in business modelling are capable of understanding more complex process models, whereas novices are not [23]. The capability to understand visualisations is measured by assessing people's visual literacy. Visual literacy is the ability and skill to read and interpret visually represented data in visualisations and extract information from them [4,15]. Visual literacy is one of the essential basic skills people need to read process models. One potential reason why experts in business modelling are more capable of understanding complex process models has to do with their perceptive and cognitive capabilities. Human perception and cognition are generally pretty fallible and have limited capacity for processing information [2]. In this study, we use a visual information modality instead of mainly textual information. Therefore, we limit the amount of information, which could make it easier to process. Another reason why experts in business modelling are more capable of understanding complex process models is that with prior learning of specific methods and patterns, they can rely on a more automatic retrieval of acquired information for understanding. These methods and patterns of prior learning suggest that a general conceptualisation of visual literacy may be shaped by education [2].

Although visualisations can improve reading and understanding of information, they can also lead to visual clutter. Visual clutter consists of either a shortage or excess of information or shortage or excess of visual properties in a graphical representation that results in a chaotic or high-density layout which creates visual complexity [2]. Additionally, this can create a lack of an organised structure for representing the data. Visual clutter has been shown to increase errors in interpretation and judgement of cluttered visualisations. However, it could increase the confidence with which people make decisions and should therefore be avoided.

One of the approaches to avoiding visual clutter is chunking. Chunking refers to grouping elements into larger or broader units based on their meaning, learnt associations or cognitive skill set [2]. In other words, segmenting complex visualisations into more manageable, meaningful chunks of information. There are different chunking strategies; in this thesis, we will focus on the perceptual chunking strategies. Perceptual chunking strategies include using common visual parameters like colour or shape [2]. Consistent use in combining these parameters can strengthen the segmentation for more efficient cognitive processing. Careful consideration about how visual display elements can be grouped into meaningful psychological entities can support perceptive and cognitive capabilities. In this study, we will be using a nudge as a form of perceptual chunking strategy to attempt to make process models more comprehensive.

According to Thaler and Sunstein [26] a nudge is any aspect of the choice architecture that predictably alters people's behaviour without forbidding any options or significantly changing their economic incentives. By adding nudges to process models, we attempt to enhance their understanding. Nudges work by targeting shortcuts within the brain when an individual needs to make a choice [11]. These shortcuts are immediate and often automatically triggered. In addition, they have no consequence for an individual's rational choice. Nudges are based on the idea that certain choices are better for an individual in the long run than others, but only when people themselves agree with the goals represented by these choices [27]. Therefore, nudges cannot be expected to change behaviours that people have strong opinions about. A strong preference in favour or against the nudged option makes the nudge ineffective. Nudges predictably influence choice behaviour and will only change contextual aspects that are presumably irrelevant [11]. With that in mind, nudges cannot take away people's freedom of choice since nudges highlight the choice context rather than forcing a specific option. Although meta-analysis and systematic reviews consistently conclude that most nudge interventions are effective, careful estimations from these publications indicate that effect sizes are small [27]. Based on this, Venema et. al. [27] conclude that nudges are particularly effective without a clear preference for a choice. Additionally, the nudge has the potential to reduce uncertainty about the choices to be made. Due to the observed lack of understanding of process models [19] and the existing experiments executed to improve this understanding thus far [12,22], we were triggered to research the benefits of nudges within the process models above changing the visual representation of the process model completely.

There are many ways a nudge can be designed; therefore, in our study, we will limit ourselves to two nudges to enhance the understanding of a process model: a colour nudge and an arrow-style nudge. We will test whether these two types of nudges affect the understanding of process models and whether they interact with visual literacy in predicting this understanding. We have chosen to use a colour nudge because the colour might make the nudge stand out from the rest of the surrounding information, making it more visually salient, which also might reduce the necessary cognitive effort needed [11]. In addition, the colour used might have a distinct effect through colour association. The reason why we have chosen to use an arrow-style nudge is because arrows engage in the process of turning informational spaces into passages [10]. An arrow takes loose bits of information and turns this information into order. With this, we hope to bring order into the process models. Combining colour and arrow style nudges can strengthen the segmentation for more efficient processing. We will investigate four conditions: a condition without a nudge, a condition with the colour nudge, a condition with the arrow nudge and a condition with the combination of both colour and arrow nudges. By using two different types of nudges and investigating the four conditions, there is a potential to get more insightful results, which could also provide better directions for future research.

To our knowledge, there is no answer in the current literature on what factors will help people enhance their understanding of process models. Some people can read visual information better than others. In this study, we investigate if nudges will help the understanding of process models, which leads to our main research question: *Will a visual nudge enhance the understanding of process models?* Based on the literature discussed, we predict that a visual nudge will have a small, significant effect to enhance the understanding of process models. Another important factor in reading process models could be the influence of visual literacy, which we will address in our first sub-question: *Will a higher visual literacy enhance the understanding of process models?* Based on the literature discussed, we predict that a higher visual literacy will significantly enhance the understanding of process models. When a visual nudge and visual literacy both enhance process models, there is a potential that there is an interaction effect, which leads us to our second sub-question: *Will there be an interaction effect between a visual nudge and visual literacy on the understanding of process models?* Based on the hypothesis of our main and first sub-question, we aim to predict an interaction effect between visual literacy and the use of nudges: we assume that people who can read process models effectively are less dependent on the nudges for their comprehension. This study's results are essential to provide helpful recommendations for improvements in the design and interpretation of process models. In other words, we will attempt to minimise the noise in the visualised message from the sender to the receiver.

2   Method

In this study, 44 participants took part, of which 37 ($N_{male} = 18$, $N_{female} = 19$, $M_{age} = 24.24$, $SD_{age} = 9.68$, range$_{age} = 18$–77) finished the entire questionnaire and were included in the results. The following demographic data were collected: gender, age, the continent on which they were raised, highest or present schooling, their employed level, their employed branch and if they were colourblind. We have collected more data using these (standardised) questionnaires than we used in the analyses, which can be used in other cross-sections but were not of interest for the research questions. In the end, not all questions were used due to the $N = 37$; therefore, we will not explain these.

This study measured two variables: visual literacy and the understanding of process models. We measured visual literacy with the Efficiency of Visual Literacy Scale (EVLS) [14]. We assessed the understanding of process models with a questionnaire designed for this study, which will be referred to as the Understanding of Process Models Scale (UPMS). Additionally, the different nudge conditions were presented within the UPMS.

The **Efficiency of Visual Literacy Scale** is a scale developed by Kiper et. al. [14] to assess students' efficiencies of visual literacy. The participants had to answer on a five-point Likert-like scale that had the following options from 1 to 5: "I can definitely not do (*Ik kan het absoluut niet doen*)", "I cannot do (*Ik kan het niet doen*)", "I can maybe do (*Ik kan het een beetje doen*)", "I can do (*Ik kan het doen*)", "I can very easily do (*Ik kan het heel gemakkelijk doen*)". Higher scores indicate higher efficiency in visual literacy. Kiper et. al. found that a 29-item and 6-factor solution was theoretically and statistically compatible for this questionnaire.

The **Understanding of Process Models Scale (UPMS)** is a questionnaire we developed for this study to assess how well people understand the information presented in a process model. The original language of the questionnaire is Dutch and consists of 10 questions and 6 process models. The participants had to answer multiple-choice questions with four possible answers per question; only one answer was considered the correct answer. The lowest score that the participants could obtain is 0, and the highest score is 13, where these higher scores indicate a better understanding of process models. Because this questionnaire was designed for this study, and this is the first time using the questionnaire, we had an expert in process models look at the questionnaire before distributing it. With the help of this expert, we have established a form of construct validity. Additionally, with the creation of the questionnaire, we created different degrees of difficulty within the questions. This way, a higher score gets harder to attain, and thus this will make a greater distinction between people who understand the process models and those who do not, within the limited amount of questions. Additionally, we added textual information to specific models to support comprehension.

We used two types of **Nudges** to enhance the understanding of process models: the colour nudge and the arrow nudge. As far as we have been able to find in the current literature, there has been no application of nudges in process models. Therefore, all our choices have been based on comparable (nudge) designs or associations and with the help and insights from experts in process modelling. In Fig. 1, 2, 3 and 4 we show an example of the same process model used in the UPMS in the different nudge conditions we made. We are aware that these nudges influence the notation definition of the visualisation and choose to ignore these definitions in this research.

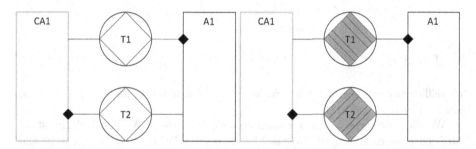

Fig. 1. No Nudge Condition Simple Process Model *Note:* The process model used in the no nudge condition of the UPMS

Fig. 2. Colour Nudge Condition Simple Process Model *Note:* The process model used in the colour nudge condition of the UPMS

First, with the colour nudge, we chose to use this nudge to determine where one could start the process model and how many times a specific element was activated during a single process instantiation. We chose the colour green for the start colour because this is a typical start colour in western society, i.e. starting lights at car races. To show how many times an element was activated, we used the colour orange and different hues of orange. An orange colour showed that the element was activated once, and a dark orange colour showed that the element was activated two times. A yellow colour showed that the element was activated under a specific condition.

Second, with the arrow nudge, we chose to use it to represent the sequence of the process model. The process model technique we used in this study was

DEMO [9]. The arrow nudge was derived from the process modelling techniques of Pronto [20] and BPMN [3]. With the visualisations of the arrow nudge, we try to bring some order into the sequence and apply those types of arrows as a nudge in the process models of DEMO to see if this would help.

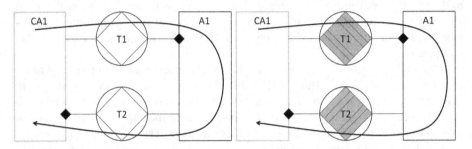

Fig. 3. Arrow Nudge Condition Simple Process Model *Note:* The process model used in the arrow nudge condition of the UPMSspace filler

Fig. 4. Arrow and Colour Nudge Condition Simple Process Model *Note:* The process model used in the arrow and colour nudge condition of the UPMS

3   Results

The Efficiency of Visual Literacy Scale (EVLS) was found to have a good internal consistency ($\alpha = .89$) [21].

We did not have a priori reason to delete outliers. We checked the standardised Understanding of Process Models Scale (UPMS) variable for potential outliers and determined an outlier as a case with a score of more than two standard deviations which identified two univariate outliers. The Mahalanobis Distance indicated that we had one multivariate outlier. In this small sample, removing the outliers was more likely to impact the potential significance. To analyse the results for the understanding of process models with and without outliers, we created four models: the first model has all cases included, the second model has the multivariate outlier excluded, the third model has the univariate outliers excluded, and the fourth model has all outliers excluded. We executed the univariate ANOVAs for the four models. The univariate ANOVA revealed no statistically significant predictor in the first or second model. In Table 1 and 2 we show the univariate ANOVAs to compare the effect of the nudges on the understanding of process models with the two nudge conditions, visual literacy and all possible interactions as predictors.

The univariate ANOVA of the third model revealed that there were statistically significant predictors. In Table 1 we show the Test of Between-Subject Effects of the ANOVA. With the two univariate outliers excluded, this model shows three significant results. The corrected model is significant (p = .036) with a large effect size (partial η^2 = .400) [7]. The ANOVA showed that the effect of visual literacy on the understanding of process models was significant (F (1,27) = 10.33, p = .003) with a large effect size (partial η^2 = .277). For a higher score on visual literacy, the participants score higher on the understanding of process models (B = .71). The ANOVA also showed that the effect of the interaction between visual literacy and the arrow nudge on the understanding of process models was significant (F (1,27) =5.37, p = .028) with a large effect size (partial η^2 = .166). The direction of the interaction effect between visual literacy and the arrow nudge on the understanding of process models was negative for the absence of the arrow nudge (B = -.36). This result means that the higher people score on visual literacy, the more they use the arrow nudge to enhance their understanding of process models. In addition, the lower people score on visual literacy, the less they use the arrow nudge to enhance their understanding of process models. The significant interaction effect from the third model is shown in Fig. 5.

Table 1. Tests of Between-Subjects Effects: Univariate outliers (2) from std. UPMS excluded

Predictor	SS	df	MS	F	p	partial η^2
Corrected Model	19.990	7	2.856	2.569	.036*	.400
Intercept	801.738	1	801.738	721.319	<,001	.964
Colour nudge (cn)	6.11E-6	1	6.11E-6	0.000	.998	.000
Arrow nudge (an)	.591	1	.591	0.532	.472	.019
Std. EVLS	11.479	1	11.479	10.328	.003*	.277
Std. EVLS*an	5.963	1	5.963	5.365	.028*	.166
Std. EVLS*cn	.408	1	.408	0.367	.550	.013
cn*an	.085	1	.085	0.077	.784	.003
Std. EVLS*cn*an	2.290	1	2.290	2.061	.164	.071

Note: The tests of between-subjects effects of the ANOVA with the univariate outliers from the std. UPMS excluded. SS = Sum of Squares; df = degrees of freedom; MS = Mean Square; F = F-value; p = significance; partial η^2 = partial Eta squared; * = $p < .05$

The univariate ANOVA of the fourth model revealed that there was a statistically significant predictor. In Table 2 we show the Test of Between-Subject Effects of the ANOVA. With all outliers excluded, this model shows one significant result. Visual literacy is a significant predictor (p = .012) with a large effect size (partial η^2 = .219) [7]. For a higher score on visual literacy, the participants score higher on the understanding of process models (B = .71).

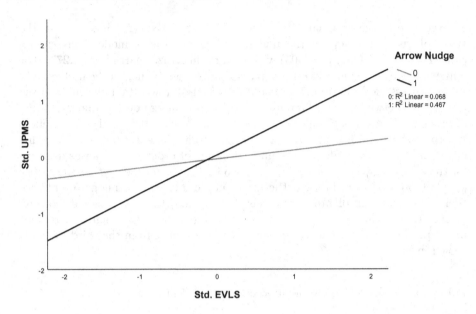

Fig. 5. Significant Interaction Effect Between Visual Literacy and the Arrow Nudge
Note: This figure shows the interaction effect between the standardised EVLS and the UPMS from the third model without the two univariate outliers. $0 =$ condition without the arrow nudge; $1 =$ condition with the arrow nudge

4   Discussion

In this study, we researched whether we could enhance the understanding of Design and Engineering Methodology for Organisations (DEMO) process models with the help of nudges, visual literacy and the interaction effects between the nudges and visual literacy. To our knowledge, there was no answer in the current literature on what factors will help with comprehension. Because of our small sample size, we analysed four different models, depending on what cases we deleted as outliers, to consider the effect of deleting the outliers on the results. The first model contains all cases; in the second model, we excluded the multi-variate outlier; in the third model, we excluded the univariate outliers; and in the fourth model, we excluded all previously determined outliers. When examining the four different models, we found that only the third and fourth models had significant predictors. Deciding whether to exclude outliers leads to conflicting results. In the paragraphs below, we will describe the interpretation of each of these results.

The sample size is the first thing we must consider when examining our results. Our sample consists of 37 complete questionnaires, 12.5% of what we needed, meaning that we do not have enough power in our analyses. Therefore, the results we have found could rest on a coincidence.

Table 2. Tests of Between-Subjects Effects: All outliers (3) excluded space filler two

Predictor	SS	df	MS	F	p	partial η^2
Corrected Model	16.031	7	2.290	1.995	.095	.349
Intercept	560.650	1	560.650	488.317	<,001	.949
Colour nudge (cn)	.051	1	.051	0.044	.835	.002
Arrow nudge (an)	.740	1	.740	0.644	.429	.024
Std. EVLS	8.382	1	8.382	7.301	.012*	.219
Std. EVLS*an	4.649	1	4.649	4.049	.055	.135
Std. EVLS*cn	.559	1	.559	0.487	.492	.018
cn*an	.216	1	.216	0.188	.668	.007
Std. EVLS*cn*an	2.048	1	2.048	1.784	.193	.064

Note: The tests of between-subjects effects of the ANOVA with all outliers excluded. SS = Sum of Squares; df = degrees of freedom; MS = Mean
Square; F = F-value; p = significance; partial η^2 = partial Eta squared;
* = $p < .05$

Firstly, we look at our main research question: *Will a visual nudge enhance
the understanding of process models?* Based on the literature discussed, we predicted that a visual nudge would have a small though significant effect on enhancing the understanding of process models. We found no significant results in our
four models for the effect of a visual nudge on the understanding of process
models, meaning that a visual nudge does not enhance the understanding of
process models based on these four models. This finding is not in line with our
expectations.

Why would the nudges not significantly affect the understanding of process
models? Besides our small sample size, different factors could influence the working of a nudge. This topic has typically been underinvestigated and systematic
groupings of relevant features are currently lacking [24]. Nonetheless, we have
four potential reasons why the nudges did not significantly affect the understanding of process models. First, when a nudge is presented, people have to observe
the nudge for the nudge to have any effect. It could have been possible that
the participants had not observed the nudge; therefore, the nudge could not aid
them in their comprehension of process models. It might help in future research
to be transparent about using nudges to ensure people observe the nudges since
transparency does not compromise nudge effects [24]. Second, the nudge being
presented is emphasising something; however, what it is emphasising concerning
the answer options could be unclear to the people. If people do not relate the
emphasis to the correct answer or not to any answers at all, then the nudges are
not functioning as we would want them to. Therefore, nudges have less effect than
anticipated. Third, we may have chosen the wrong nudges to enhance people's
understanding of process models in this situation. There are many dimensions
(e.g. spatial and chromatic) on which we can design a nudge [16]. Because we
had to limit ourselves in this study, we selected two kinds of nudges. However,

there is a possibility that a different kind of nudge works better than the ones we selected. Another possibility for a different kind of nudge could be a change within the dimension, i.e. using a different colour, or a change in the use of the dimension, i.e. using a nudge on the orientation dimension instead of the spatial dimension. Fourth and last, not only is the kind of nudge of potential influence, but the placement of the nudge could also be of influence. The placement of the nudge within the process model is related to the context. There is no neutral choice context; a new choice context or a change in the choice context may bring higher costs than leaving it be [13]. Therefore, the nudge may have been placed in a position that changed the model so that it did not optimally support the comprehension. Even more so, the nudge may have added to confusion instead of comprehension because of this change in context. Considering these potential explanations, nudges could be significant on their own.

Secondly, we look at our first sub-question: *Will a higher visual literacy enhance the understanding of process models?* Based on the literature discussed, we predicted that a higher visual literacy would significantly enhance the understanding of process models. In the first and second models, we did not find a significant result for the effect of visual literacy on the understanding of process models. In the third and fourth models, we did find a significant result for the effect of visual literacy on the understanding of process models. Because of our small sample size, all our results could rest on a coincidence. On the one hand, our lack of finding significant results in the first and second models is contrary to our expectations. Visuals play a significant role in learning and performance and have to be planned and used purposefully to communicate the intended message [1]. A potential explanation for not finding a significant result could be that the process model was not designed in a way that it communicated the intended message. Therefore, it could be too difficult to read, regardless of whether people had a high visual literacy. Additionally, it could be that the scale we chose to measure visual literacy was not suitable for this situation. On the other hand, in the third and fourth models, we found significant results that were in line with our expectations. A potential explanation for finding significant results could be because of visual literacy itself. Visual literacy is acquired competencies for interpreting visual messages [1]. Visual literacy is one of the essential basic skills people need to read visuals [4,15]. Therefore, this essential skill could explain the significant results found in the third and fourth models.

Lastly, we look at the second sub-question: *Will there be an interaction effect between a visual nudge and visual literacy on the understanding process models?* Based on the hypothesis of our main and first sub-question, we aimed to predict an interaction effect between visual literacy and the use of nudges: we assumed that people who can read process models effectively are less dependent on the nudges for their comprehension. The first, second and fourth models showed no significant interaction effects. This result was not in line with our expectations. The third model did show a significant interaction effect. However, this interaction was in the opposite direction of what we expected. We expected an interaction effect where people who score higher on visual literacy are less dependent on the visual nudges for their understanding of process models. However, the interaction effect showed that people who score higher on visual literacy profit more from the arrow nudge for their understanding of process models. Therefore, this result was not in line with our expectations. A potential explanation for these results could be that the type of nudges we used had no relation to visual literacy.

Furthermore, in the third model, the corrected model shows an explained variance of partial $\eta^2 = .400$, which means that the corrected model explains 40% of the variance for the understanding of process models. According to Cohen [7] this is a large effect. Venema et. al. [27] described with careful estimations that the effect sizes of nudges are small; therefore, we expected a small effect within this study. Since we did not find a small effect but a large effect in the third model, we have to wonder why we found this large effect. A potential explanation for this finding concerns the significance found in the predictors of this model. We did not find any significant nudging predictors. However, we did find a significant result for the visual literacy predictor and the interaction between visual literacy and the arrow nudge, suggesting that the high explained variance is due to visual literacy, not the nudges. This assumption is also confirmed by the explained variance of the visual literacy predictor, which also has a large effect (partial $\eta^2 = .277$).

The following methodological limitations could have affected this research. First, as mentioned earlier, our sample size was 37 participants. The sample size needed we have calculated by using G*Power (Version 3). According to those calculations, we needed 295 participants when calculating with an effect size of 0.05. Our sample size turned out to be 12.5% of the sample size we needed to collect based on the calculations of G*Power. Despite the significance of the third model, because of the small sample size ($N = 37$), we cannot claim any power. Therefore, the significance found in the third model could rest on a coincidence.

Second, the amount of highly educated students (HBO and WO[1]) in the sample ($\approx 83\%$) is disproportionate the to actual population ($\approx 24\%$ [6]) in the same age group. Because of this enormous difference, it becomes more challenging to generalise and accurately picture the current results. Additionally, this could mean that results could be more skewed towards the top scores due to the high schooling in the current sample than they would be if the sample were more representative of the schooling level of the population in the Netherlands.

Third, the sample comprises only people with an employment level under C-level. In Mulder [19] it is stated that the comprehension of process models is, in practice, experienced as more of a problem on the employment level of C-level. A C-level executive (e.g. CEO, CFO, CTO) is a person who holds a senior position, plays a strategic role within the organisation, and impacts company-wide decisions. With this sample, we cannot state conclusions about the people who function on a C-level.

---

[1] University of Applied Science and University in international terms.

Fourth, we used a form of self-report (questionnaire), using the Efficiency of Visual Literacy Scale (EVLS), to attain the results. Questionnaires rely on truthful responses from participants to draw meaningful conclusions [18]. When participants do not answer accurately, they may believe the answer they report is accurate (self-deception) or may 'fake good' or 'fake bad' [18]. Thus, there may be socially desirable response bias in the results of the EVLS which could mean that the results are potentially more skewed towards higher scores on the EVLS in this sample because people want to believe or present that they are good at visual literacy.

Fifth and last, we used multiple choice answers in the Understanding of Process Models Scale (UPMS). Using multiple-choice answers could increase the chance of correct answers without the participant knowing the answer. In other words, there is a 25% betting odds of getting the correct answer. We could have applied a correction for betting odds; however, due to time restrictions, we did not. We choose multiple choice instead of open questions because open questions are harder to interpret.

5 Future Research

This study's results are essential to provide helpful recommendations for improvements in the design and interpretation of process models. We conjecture that enhancing visual literacy is more profitable than adding nudges to process models where as the interaction effects of the nudges on process models have been over estimated.

Based on this research we recommend further research on enhancing the understanding of process models. Firstly, we could combine the need for education with the necessity to read the process model and include the education of visual literacy in process model legends. This option, that needs a lot of further research, would help new people in the field to directly connect to the information in the process model while experienced people are not scared away by 'childish' additions to model visualisations. Secondly, Alhadad [2] claims that the importance of education in shaping visualisation and visual literacy cannot be understated. With the potential significant result from visual literacy and the large effect size, this could be an important direction in general. All visualisation is based on shared conventions that make up how people construct and interpret messages [5], by educating people in business process models we could create a shared convention. Thirdly, a next step in this research is to look at both quantitative and qualitative evidence [2]. To talk with people, ask them what they think is needed to enhance the understanding of process models. This way, we could get more insight into the reader's experience. By embedding future model in a concrete business case we can collect more accurate results, thereby improving the quality of the results we collect. Fourthly, we recommend that in future research, we investigate whether schooling groups other than HBO and WO arrive in jobs that require the kind of visual literacy needed with reading process models. When researching this, we can discern if people in higher education are the more important group when it comes to enhancing process models.

Lastly, from a psychological point of view, more research into the workings of nudges could be done with focus on which factors determine whether nudges will influence people in general [24]. This research is essential because, as mentioned before, this topic has been underinvestigated and is currently lacking. Therefore, in future research, one can give more attention to visual literacy in education and in visualisations itself.

In future research, we recommend addressing the following methodologically concerns. First, we recommend more focus on collecting a representative sample; this will hopefully create results that can be generalised and show an accurate picture of the situation. Second and last, in contrast to self-report, a different form of data collection of visual literacy might yield more evident results, leading to less potential bias.

In conclusion, we have conjectured that good visual literacy exceeds the interaction effects of nudges. Further research can reveal whether we can find a path on which people will better understand process modelling in the context of Enterprise Engineering (EE) in general and DEMO process models in particular within the process model documentation itself.

References

1. Aisami, R.S.: Learning styles and visual literacy for learning and performance. Procedia-Soc. Behav. Sci. **176**, 538–545 (2015). https://doi.org/10.1016/j.sbspro.2015.01.508
2. Alhadad, S.S.: Visualizing data to support judgement, inference, and decision making in learning analytics: insights from cognitive psychology and visualization science. J. Learn. Anal. **5**(2), 60–85 (2018). https://doi.org/10.18608/jla.2018.52.5
3. Allweyer, T.: BPMN 2.0: introduction to the standard for business process modeling. BoD-Books on Demand (2016)
4. Börner, K., Bueckle, A., Ginda, M.: Data visualization literacy: definitions, conceptual frameworks, exercises, and assessments. Proc. Natl. Acad. Sci. **116**(6), 1857–1864 (2019). https://doi.org/10.1073/pnas.1807180116
5. Card, S.K., Mackinlay, J.D.S.B.: Readings in Information Visualization: Using Vision to Think. Morgan Kaufmann Publishers, San Francisco (1999)
6. Centraal Bureau voor de Statistiek: Bevolking 15 tot 75 jaar; opleidingsniveau, wijken en buurten, 2020 (2021). https://opendata.cbs.nl/statline/#/CBS/nl/dataset/85051NED/table?ts=1654936548110
7. Cohen, J.: Statistical power analysis for the behavioral sciences (1988)
8. Dewan, P.: Words versus pictures: leveraging the research on visual communication. Partnership Can. J. Libr. Inf. Pract. Res. **10**(1) (2015). https://doi.org/10.21083/partnership.v10i1.3137
9. Dietz, J., Mulder, H.: Enterprise Ontology: A Human-Centric Approach to Understanding the Essence of Organisation. Springer, Heidelberg (2020)
10. Fuller, G.: The arrow-directional semiotics: wayfinding in transit. Social Semiot, **12**(3), 231–244 (2002). https://doi.org/10.1080/10350330216376
11. Fyhri, A., Karlsen, K., Sundfør, H.B.: Paint it red-a multimethod study of the nudging effect of coloured cycle lanes. Front. Psychol. **12** (2021). https://doi.org/10.3389/fpsyg.2021.662679

12. Gouveia, B., Aveiro, D., Pacheco, D., Pinto, D., Gouveia, D.: Fact model in DEMO - urban law case and proposal of representation improvements. In: Aveiro, D., Guizzardi, G., Pergl, R., Proper, H.A. (eds.) EEWC 2020. LNBIP, vol. 411, pp. 173–190. Springer, Cham (2021). https://doi.org/10.1007/978-3-030-74196-9_10

13. Grill, K.: Expanding the nudge: designing choice contexts and choice contents. Rational. Mark. Morals **5**, 139–162 (2014)

14. Kiper, A., Arslan, S., Kıyıcı, M., Akgün, Ö.E.: Visual literacy scale: the study of validity and reliability. Online J. New Horiz. Educ. **2**(2), 73–83 (2012)

15. Lee, S., Kim, S.H., Kwon, B.C.: Vlat: development of a visualization literacy assessment test. IEEE Trans. Vis. Comput. Graph. **23**(1), 551–560 (2016). https://doi.org/10.1109/TVCG.2016.2598920

16. Marchak, F.M., Cleveland, W.S., Rogowitz, B.E., Wickens, C.D.: The psychology of visualization. In: IEEE Visualization: Proceedings of the 4th conference on Visualization 1993, San Jose, California, vol. 25, pp. 351–354 (1993)

17. Moody, D.: The "physics" of notations: toward a scientific basis for constructing visual notations in software engineering. IEEE Trans. Softw. Eng. **35**(6), 756–779 (2009). https://doi.org/10.1109/TSE.2009.67

18. Van de Mortel, T.F.: Faking it: social desirability response bias in self-report research. Aust. J. Adv. Nurs. **25**(4), 40–48 (2008)

19. Mulder, M.A.T.: A design evaluation of an extension to the DEMO methodology. In: Aveiro, D., Guizzardi, G., Borbinha, J. (eds.) EEWC 2019. LNBIP, vol. 374, pp. 55–65. Springer, Cham (2020). https://doi.org/10.1007/978-3-030-37933-9_4

20. Noorman, B.: Pronto: Bpm-aanpak van sogeti (2008). https://docplayer.nl/15621365-White-paper-pronto-bpm-aanpak-sogeti-auteur-bert-noorman.html

21. Nunnally, J., Bernstein, I.: Psychometric Theory. McGraw-Hill, New york (1994)

22. Pinto, D., Aveiro, D., Pacheco, D., Gouveia, B., Gouveia, D.: Validation of DEMO's conciseness quality and proposal of improvements to the process model. In: Aveiro, D., Guizzardi, G., Pergl, R., Proper, H.A. (eds.) EEWC 2020. LNBIP, vol. 411, pp. 133–152. Springer, Cham (2021). https://doi.org/10.1007/978-3-030-74196-9_8

23. Reijers, H.A., Mendling, J.: A study into the factors that influence the understandability of business process models. IEEE Trans. Syst. Man Cybern. Part A: Syst. Hum. **41**(3), 449–462 (2011). https://doi.org/10.1109/TSMCA.2010.2087017

24. de Ridder, D., Kroese, F., van Gestel, L.: Nudgeability: mapping conditions of susceptibility to nudge influence. Perspect. Psychol. Sci. **17**(2), 346–359 (2022). https://doi.org/10.1177/1745691621995183

25. Schnotz, W.: An integrated model of text and picture comprehension. Cambridge Handbook Multimedia Learn. **49**, 69 (2005)

26. Thaler, R., Sunstein, C.: Nudge: Improving Decisions About Health, Wealth and Happiness. The Final Edition, Allen Lane (2021)

27. Venema, T.A., Kroese, F.M., Benjamins, J.S., de Ridder, D.T.: When in doubt, follow the crowd? responsiveness to social proof nudges in the absence of clear preferences. Front. Psychol. **11**, 1385 (2020). https://doi.org/10.3389/fpsyg.2020.01385

28. Ware, C.: Information Visualization: Perception for Design. Academic Press, San Diego (2004)

Towards a Reference Architecture for Planning and Control Services

Mohammad Pourmehdi$^{(\boxtimes)}$, Maria E. Iacob , and Martijn R. K. Mes

University of Twente, Drienerlolaan 5, 7522 NB Enschede, The Netherlands
{m.pourmehdi,m.e.iacob,m.r.k.mes}@utwente.nl

Abstract. Producers of manufacturing equipment can, instead of just selling their products, also offer their customers services to increase customer satisfaction, gain competitive advantage, and increase their profits. These goals can be reached by helping the customers optimise their processes and improve their reliability and flexibility. This can be done by supporting the customer that invests in new manufacturing machines with a planning and control tool connecting the machines and the processes between them. More specifically, this will become possible by introducing and integrating active data management and analysis, and planning applications in the current architecture of companies. All of the processes currently being done manually in the customer companies, from monitoring to production planning based on direct observation and the experience of production managers, can be automated using these applications. This paper presents a reference architecture supporting the connection of these processes using the mentioned applications, and validates the developed models based on a real case study of a production machine manufacturer and its customers.

Keywords: Service provision · Manufacturing machines · Reference architecture · Production planning · Data management

1 Introduction

Nowadays, customers prefer suppliers that can provide specific accompanying services to their offering items, not those that sell mere products or equipment [1]. Therefore, a production machine manufacturer that can offer specific and customised services helping their customers in various stages of using their purchased equipment is a priority choice for the customers [2]. Hence, it is logical for equipment manufacturers to start an initiative offering customised services [3]. There are several types of services that companies can offer their customers, helping them in managing their processes in different ways and degrees. Depending on the company, the customers might not like to give full access of their processes to their suppliers and become completely reliant on them. Hence they would be more interested in services offered through the use of software or an artefact helping them with efficient connection and utilisation of the equipment they purchased, aiming to manage and optimise their use [4].

The service provision initiative will result in increased customer satisfaction [5, 6] and also create competitive advantages [7, 8]. Subsequently, from these gains, the

C. Griffo et al. (Eds.): EEWC 2022, LNBIP 473, pp. 121–138, 2023.
https://doi.org/10.1007/978-3-031-34175-5_8

service provider will get closer to its final goal, increasing the total profit [9, 10]. One of the main ways to support the customer companies by presenting them a service to enhance their experience using the equipment they purchased is by helping them using the equipment efficiently and effectively, increasing the flexibility and reliability of their production systems [11, 12]. One of the ways to define the offering service is that this service will help the customer companies move toward automation and elimination of manual processes as much as possible. This can be done using dynamic and efficient production planning approaches, helping them use their purchased equipment efficiently and effectively [13, 14].

Customer companies can move towards their goals by aligning their business needs and information systems throughout different levels of their operations, aiming to control and optimise their processes. The business question is what kinds of services the service-providing companies should offer to their customers. Also, they should find the best way to offer these services to their customers, supporting the efficient and effective use of purchased machines, helping them to reach their goals in their factory control and optimisation process. In more detail, they can illustrate the expected results of this integration process and how it will affect the current architecture of the customer companies.

The enterprise architecture discipline presents a shared language for building efficient guidelines for such an integration [15]. The shared modelling language encompasses the concepts related to information technology (IT) systems and their applications alongside the physical environment for presenting a blueprint for the integration process, which can be called a reference architecture (RA) [16]. Kruchten [17] defines the RA: "A reference architecture is, in essence, a predefined architectural pattern, or set of patterns, possibly partially or completely instantiated, designed and proven for use, in particular, business and technical contexts, together with supporting artefacts to enable their use. Often, these artefacts are harvested from previous projects." Another definition of a reference model is a conceptual framework that describes a collection of connecting ideas and relationships regardless of specific standards, technologies, or implementations within a specific problem domain [18]. Hence, based on the presented definitions for an RA, this study considers the use of RAs to create guidelines for incorporating a control and optimisation toolbox into the current architecture of customer companies of production machines and analysing its influence on their architecture as the research problem.

This study is structured based on the research methodology for research in information systems suggested by Peffers et al. [19]. The research methodology and how each section of this paper is aligned with the methodology are shown in Fig. 1. The following sections focus on the literature review and the research gap (Sect. 2), motivation and strategy analysis (Sect. 3), model design (Sect. 4), discussion and case study (Sect. 5), and conclusion and further research (Sect. 6).

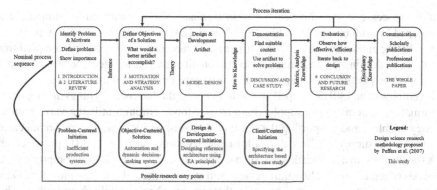

Fig. 1. Research methodology

2   Literature Review

The literature review is divided into two parts: (i) servitisation and (ii) RAs, highlighting the importance of servitisation for companies and the application of RAs.

Servitisation in manufacturing companies is defined as the process of enhancing the capabilities of a company to provide a better experience for its final customers and increasing the revenue streams for both stakeholders by offering specific services [20]. Gebauer et al. [21] performed a literature review focusing on the contributions of the service strategies. They also presented guidelines for managers in manufacturing companies interested in offering services related to the products they sell in several industries. Kohtamäki et al. [22] analysed the correlation between service offering and sales growth. The results, according to the data collected from multiple Finnish manufacturers, showed a non-linear relationship between sales growth and service offering. A study extending the service levels by adding a new type of service to a product-service value chain to increase the long-term competitive advantages of the chain was performed by Opresnik and Taisch [23]. They concluded that this idea would increase the competitive advantages and revenue streams for the service provider and customer. Tenucci and Supino [24] examined the correlation between profitability and different types of product-service systems. The findings of the empirical analysis revealed that when companies focus on both product and service, they have higher profitability than the case of focus on one of them. Zhang et al. [25] analysed the facilitating influence of technology and market orientation strategies on different levels of service provision types relative to variable firm sizes. They conducted an empirical study using survey data confirming that service provision significantly improves the sustainable profile of manufacturers.

Recent studies that designed RAs and highlighted their application are presented in the following. Iacob et al. [26] presented an architecture for a fuel-based carbon emission calculation system collecting real-time data during trips of vehicles using onboard computers. The designed system also integrated the business processes of logistics service providers and typical software applications. Hernández et al. [27] suggested a novel RA to support cooperative decision-making in the supply chain. The architecture was validated through its application in an automotive supply chain where improvements in service levels were observed. An RA addressing customers and business partners in the internal processes of the whole enterprise in the field of service-oriented e-commerce was developed by Aulkemeier et al. [28]. Singh et al. [29] proposed an integration platform RA assisting enterprises in making affirmative decisions regarding integration platform solutions or design. The research did a commonality analysis to select the best practices in integration platform design and act as a reference point for future research.

Verdouw et al. [30] developed an RA to integrate the Internet of Things and logistics information systems in the supply chain of agri-food. Through utilising various technology enablers and supporting the reuse of domain-specific features, the architecture facilitates the supply of affordable tailor-made solutions. Iacob et al. [31] proposed an RA for situation-aware logistics based on the principles extracted from a comprehensive analysis of requirements, literature review, and the prompted idea by the Industrial Data Space initiative. A study proposing an RA that aims to enhance supply chain resilience by relying on Smart Logistics and the Internet of Things was done by Koot et al. [32]. They included a hierarchical set of disruption handling mechanisms to enhance the analysis of the trade-off between response time and decision quality in their model.

Based on the literature review on servitisation, the increasing value of adding services next to offering products by a company in different areas of industry can be highlighted. Also, based on the review regarding enterprise architecture and RAs, it has been noted that having concrete and generalised plans for integrating different principles and processes in a system can enhance the integration process and guarantee its final success. The benefits of adding different types of services alongside the selling products of a company are noted by multiple studies; however, there are no guidelines on how a company can start offering such services to their customers.

The contribution of this research can be highlighted in facilitating the efficient planning and control of production lines, meaning that the study focuses on the successful integration of planning and control services in manufacturing companies using enterprise engineering concepts. To the best of our knowledge, according to the state of the art, there is no guideline such as an RA for this phenomenon. The lack of an RA, used as a guideline for companies that intend to add a planning toolbox as a service to the products they sell, is part of the research gap we are focusing on. Hence, the contribution of this study is designing a reference model for the mentioned phenomenon based on the ArchiMate® 3.1 Specification [33] to fill the existing knowledge gap and integrate optimisation and control approaches, as a part of the planning toolbox, with the company architecture as an active system. The presented models are also validated using a real case study at a manufacturing company of production machines intending to offer control and planning services to their customers.

3   Motivation and Strategy Analysis

An important characteristic of an RA is to act as a reference to ease the communication of a technical design among the stakeholders. This is often accomplished using an abstract representation of the system using architectural perspectives, which show the system in a context relevant to the needs and goals of stakeholders [34]. One of the main challenges in collaborative projects is to convey the main idea and reason behind a collaboration between business and technical stakeholders using different languages [35].

Since the goal is to provide data standards, services, and process plans at the enterprise level, clarity for all stakeholders associated with the architectural definitions and design becomes critical [36]. The ability of stakeholders to have a complete understanding of the potential of each prospective project, next to the ability of the architects of those systems to effectively incorporate business strategies into the architectural design, will determine whether they succeed or fail [34]. An RA should highlight the link between business motivations, strategies, services, processes, and the information to support those strategies and motivations [37].

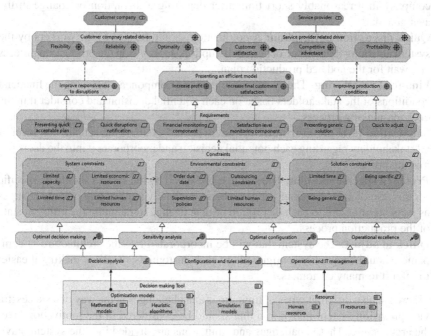

Fig. 2. Motivation and strategy layers

The necessity of designing such a system to provide the required services can be highlighted by presenting the motivation and strategy view of the proposed integration architecture. The motivation and strategy view of this study is presented in Fig. 2. The figure is designed based on literature and interviews with industry managers. According to the name and the colour of the elements in the figure, it can be seen that this view of the architecture is divided into two parts: (i) motivation and (ii) strategy.

The motivation layer consists of the stakeholders, drivers, goals, requirements, and constraints. The stakeholders of the suggested integration are the service-providing company and the customer companies of the service [38]. Each of these stakeholders has their specific drivers in mind to be interested in this integration. These drivers are formed following the requirements that the to-be-designed tool should satisfy. The drivers for the service-providing company are increasing their profit and the satisfaction of their final customers. Increasing customer satisfaction will be achieved by providing a service that helps the customers achieve their own drivers [39–41].

The requirements that should be satisfied by the target architecture are mentioned briefly in Fig. 2, at the fourth level of the motivation and strategy view. The requirements are formed based on interviews with several industry managers from the service-providing company and their potential customer companies, asking them about their needs and then translating them to the requirements the proposed service provision initiative should satisfy [42]. The details of these requirements are mentioned in the following.

- **Present a quick plan:** The system should update the production plan of the customer company in a reasonably short time after detecting a disruption or change in the available data.
- **Quick disruption notification:** A notification should be sent to the workers by the system notifying them of the occurred disruption, so they stop the production process and wait for the updated production plan.
- **Financial monitoring:** The system should have a component analysing the financial conditions of the stakeholders based on each potential decision and consider it in the decision-making process.
- **Satisfaction level monitoring:** The system should evaluate the satisfaction level of all stakeholders regarding each potential decision and incorporate it into the decision-making process.
- **Present a specific solution:** The solution presented by the system should be specific for the case of each customer, so it can be immediately applied without any changes as a countermeasure to each disruption or data change to maintain the efficient state of the production process.
- **Quick to adjust:** The system that will be incorporated into the architecture of companies should be quickly configurable to each customer's situation, making it easier to offer it to many customers.

There are also different types of limitations and challenges in the way of a successful service provision system integration that should be considered in the motivation layer of the architecture. These challenges and limitations are divided into the system, environmental, and solution constraints. System and environmental constraints are enforced by the conditions of the customer company and the conditions, laws, and regulations of different countries or states, respectively. Examples of system constraints are that the company has limited capacity and human resources, which should be considered so the solution presented by the system would not offer to use another machine for a specific process or add another worker to a workstation to finish the job without considering the extra cost and the changes it will impose to the company. Limitations in the availability of the workforce in an area of work in a specific region or not being allowed to use a specific technology or purchase a particular type of raw material are the constraints enforced by the environment.

The solution constraints are associated with the dynamic decision-making software of the target architecture, which guarantee the efficiency of the presented solution [43–46]. For example, being generic and specific means that the software should be generic enough to be configurable for different companies, but have the required configuration parameters, to make it specific for each company.

The strategy layer is divided into resource, capability, and course of action. The required resources for the suggested integration have specific capabilities, which result in the specified course of actions affecting the realisation of the motivation layer. The resources are divided into human and IT resources, assigned to operational and IT management to realise operational excellence [47, 48]. The other part of the resources is the to-be-developed tool assigned to configuration and rule-setting, and decision analysis, realising optimal configuration, sensitivity analysis, and optimal decisions [49–51]. The decision-making tool would work as the primary enabler of this service provision initiative.

4   Model Design

In this section, we first present the baseline architecture, which shows the current conditions of the customer companies of production machines without receiving the offered service. After that, the target architecture is developed based on the presented motivation and strategy view. The target architecture shows how the stakeholders reach their desired goals by adding the control and optimisation toolbox to the enterprise. Table 1 presents the main concepts used in the designed models, accompanied by a short description of them.

Table 1. Definitions of concepts used in the presented model

Concept	Definition
System	All of the components (micro-systems) and processes of the customer company that interact with each other and work to produce the final product
Solution	A complete production plan, consisting of the purchasing of raw materials, production sequences, and scheduling of the processes of the system
Machine	Production machines purchased from the service-providing company, used in the customer company for the production process
Disruption	Any type of event that can halt the production process and requires change of the production plan
Dynamic operation planning	Changing the production plan according to the occurrence of disruptions or a change in order details, which requires an updated plan for maintaining the production process in an efficient state
Model (Technology layer)	The decision-making process used for presenting and updating the solution based on the condition of the system at any moment in time

The presented models are developed based on interviews with production managers of a few collaborating service-providing and customer companies. The focus of the interviews was on gaining insight into the details of the current and ideal collaboration between these companies. Moreover, the discussions revolved around how these companies function in the current conditions, in which areas they require improvements, and the ideal picture they have in their mind for their future production process.

4.1 Baseline Model

The baseline architecture shown in Fig. 3 represents the typical architecture of the control and optimisation process of customer companies that buy production machines without any accompanying services. More specifically, this applies to companies that currently do not have a toolbox for synchronised and real-time monitoring and optimisation of their processes. Hence, these processes are done by the managers of these companies using simple tools based on experience and limited data. These companies have the characteristics of a flexible or hybrid flow shop where the workload between the different stages of the production process should be balanced to have efficient performance. All production stages should be actively connected and share information to achieve maximum synchronisation between the stages, which is absent in the current architecture of our target companies.

The main stakeholders of the control and optimisation application are the manufacturing companies and the final customers of their products. The customer company itself is responsible for operations management and monitoring services. The production planning process is triggered by the production planning application or the disruption detection event. Due to the absence of an advanced real-time data management system, the disruption detection event leads to notifying the managers, and after that, the countermeasure, e.g., in terms of providing materials or performing a repair, is done by operators based on the decision made by the managers. The disruption readiness and system optimisation functions realise the operations monitoring and management services, respectively, enabling the company to serve its final customers.

The data management and production planning application components both function using spreadsheet applications. These applications are responsible for data aggregation and storage, and present production plans, and through that, realise the data and system management services. The data management application has access to order details, supply, delivery, and production line data. This application also serves the production planning application, which itself functions through the management software interface. The technology layer of the architecture consists of a computer device with an operating system and spreadsheet software to realise decision-making and monitoring services. The production machines and, within them, the safety and operational sensors have data flow to the computers and are also associated with production line data.

The baseline architecture shows that there is room for improvement in the functioning of the operations and the data sharing in the customer company aiming to reach the drivers and goals mentioned in the motivation and strategy view of the architecture. There are specific guidelines required for a successful upgrade of the system, which might require the assistance of external parties and upgrading the equipment of the company.

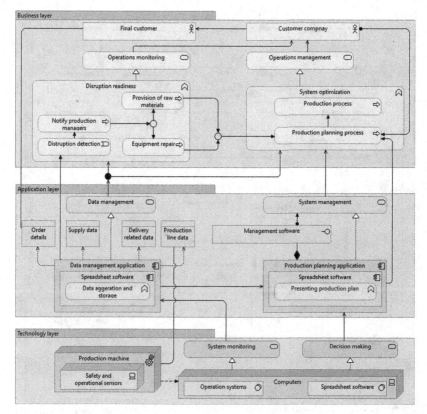

Fig. 3. Baseline architecture

4.2 Target Model

Based on the definitions of RAs, they are generic designs that can be made specific to several cases based on adding further specifications to the models [52]. The vision and logic behind the target architecture design is to create a guide or blueprint for the service-providing and customer companies, assisting them through the collaboration. This initiative leads to offering the factory control and optimisation toolbox by the service provider to the customer companies to reach their drivers and goals mentioned in the motivation and strategy view of the architecture in Fig. 2.

The main changes in the target architecture compared to the baseline are set in motion by designing and adding the dynamic decision-making software to the architecture and adding the service provider as a stakeholder. The dynamic decision-making software will be developed by the service-providing company specifically for each industry with several configurable parameters that help the customer companies of the software to use the services in their company after adjusting it to their conditions. All changes after adding these elements are shown in Fig. 4, and some of the major ones are explored in the following.

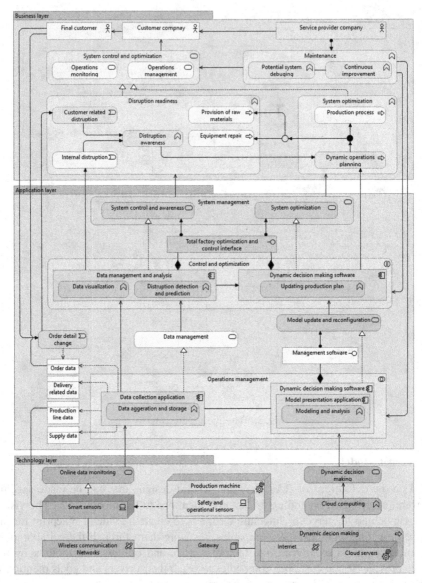

Fig. 4. Target architecture

Adding the service-providing company as a stakeholder will add some functions to the business layer, serving the operation management and monitoring services. The functions assigned to the service-providing company are potential debugging and continuous improvements of their designed application, which serve the system control and optimisation service assigned to the customer company. These connections show that the service-providing company is helping its customer to control and optimise the production processes of the customer company. In the target architecture, the dynamic production planning is triggered by the dynamic decision-making software or the disruption aware-ness function. The disruption awareness itself is triggered by customer-related or internal disruption events, which will be explored in detail when discussing the application layer.

The structure of the application layer is almost completely changed due to adding the dynamic decision-making software to the architecture. System management service, which consists of system optimisation, and system control and awareness services, is the main component that serves the business layer. This layer also has two added application collaborations with different functions. The first one is operation management collabo-ration consisting of a data collection application and dynamic decision-making software with data aggregation and storage as well as modelling and analysis functions. The sec-ond collaboration is control and optimisation, which consists of data management and analysis and dynamic decision-making software. In this collaboration, the data man-agement and analysis application can trigger the dynamic decision-making software updating the production plan. Also, the data management and analysis application is served by the data collection application accessing the order data. Hence, the changes in order data that can come from the customer in the middle of the production process can change the production plan and require and result in an updated plan that the dynamic decision-making software will present.

The technology services will be changed to online data monitoring and dynamic decision-making to serve the new application layer. The dynamic decision-making ser-vice is achieved using cloud computing, which requires cloud servers to transfer data through the internet, and the online data monitoring service requires smart sensors. Also, the internet, gateway, wireless connection networks, and smart sensors are all associ-ated together to serve the technology services. These changes will make data sharing between different production stages possible and improve production planning and dis-ruption readiness. Moreover, these improvements will balance the workload, resulting in an efficient production process. Since the presented architectures only focus on the most common processes and sections of the companies that require production machines for their processing, they are in a generic state that can represent the defined types of companies in different industries.

5 Discussion and Case Study

This section presents a discussion of the research and the case study used to validate it. The motivation and strategy view presented in this study indicate the primal demand for the design of a system that can automate the operations monitoring and management of the production process in manufacturing companies. Since the companies that acquire their production machines from a supplier, such a supplier can also design and offer these management systems to the customers to increase their customer satisfaction, compet-itive advantage, and profit. However, the design and implementation of the suggested system in different industries might require the extension or simplification of some parts of the presented architectures.

The reference architecture shown in Fig. 4 aims to increase the reliability, flexibility, and efficiency of the performance of the production process of companies that intend to use the introduced service. The introduced service will achieve the mentioned goals by changing the architecture to the target model by incorporating real-time data collection and dynamic decision-making for the production process. The disruption awareness function is also added to the architecture, which leads to real-time changes in the production plan in case of internal or customer-related disruptions detected by the data management and analysis application. Hence, the influence of humans is reduced from the monitoring and decision-making processes resulting in reduced human errors, delays in notifying managers and operators, and the time required for the decision-making process.

In this section, a case study consisting of a service-providing company and one of its customers from the production machine manufacturing industry has been selected to analyse the effects of designing and adding such a system to the current collaboration of these companies. The presented models in the study are designed based on the gathered information from multiple customer companies with different sizes and characteristics, and even located in different countries, however, all in the same industry track. These interviews focused more on the detail of the interactions of the different elements of the business layers of these companies to understand better their current condition and how they would function in the ideal conditions. The other potential case studies of this research can be selected between the companies that require production machines for a part of their production process, while the machines have no integrated system. A system that connects all machines and processes together, collecting real-time data for active planning and disruption management. The limitation of the presented architecture is that there are no specific details regarding what is happening inside the dynamic decision-making software. The reason is that this software would have different characteristics for each specific industry, and adding them to the models would reduce their generic characteristics. This means that even though it has been tried to present models as generic as possible, there could be some cases that would not fit into the category of the mentioned companies, meaning that the models should be modified further to apply to those cases.

To go into more detail on how the different parts of the architecture of the associated companies would be affected when receiving the mentioned services, one specific service-providing company and one of its customers are selected to make the generic models more specific and see the applicability of the presented models. The considered service-providing company has sold several production machines to the customer company of the case study, and now they intend to design a toolbox application with the mentioned functions in the target architecture to be used at the customer company. The customer produces several types of products using its purchased automatic production machines, followed by an interactive human-machine workshop assembling the half-finished products produced as the outflow of the production machines. The first workshop has the characteristics of a flexible or hybrid flow shop, and the second workshop has the characteristics of a job shop workshop. These two workshops should be connected, and the workload between them should be balanced for efficient production.

In more detail, this section focuses on analysing the changes in the business processes of the customer company after using the designed system through the extended business layer views for the baseline and target models. As mentioned, these models are designed in collaboration with experts from the selected production machine manufacturer as the service-providing company and customer companies of their machines. The business

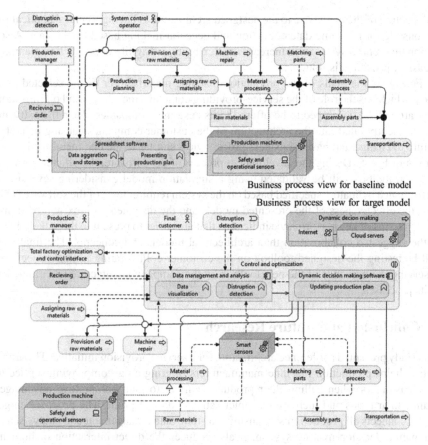

Business process view for baseline model

Business process view for target model

Fig. 5. Business process views

process view for the baseline and target models are presented in the top and bottom parts of Fig. 5, respectively. The main element of the business view for the baseline model is the system control operator, who is assigned to almost all processes for operations monitoring and, subsequently, disruption detection. The production planning in the baseline model is triggered when receiving an order and by the production manager. As presented in the model, the data management system does not influence any processes and functions because it only collects data and only has limited data inflows from different processes. This makes production planning and monitoring relatively slow and vulnerable to human errors.

On the other hand, when looking at the business process view for the target model, it can be seen that the human factors responsible for monitoring and decision-making have been eliminated, and the control and optimisation application is now responsible for all processes. This application interaction consists of data management and analytics, and dynamic decision-making software. The dynamic decision-making software triggers all business processes, and the data management and analysis application receives data from them, making the production process interconnected. Hence, the advantage of developing the structure of the enterprise to the designed architecture is having a central application responsible for real-time data collection and decision-making based on the data. Also, having this central system will increase the flexibility and agility of production planning in case of possible disruptions.

Following the goals of the production machine manufacturer of the selected case study, which has the role of the service-providing company, the control and optimisation software will be developed to be offered to its customer companies. Then the software will be incorporated into the architecture of the customer companies causing its architecture to change and have a business process view similar to the one mentioned at the bottom of Fig. 5. During the development process of the software, the efficiency of the designed toolbox will be validated using a simulation model considering several key performance indicators specified based on the system requirements of the software. This way, the effectiveness of the presented models and the designed toolbox will be translated in terms of key performance indicators that are easier to present to the stakeholders of the suggested collaboration than architectural models and concepts. The final step will be testing the designed toolbox on the customer collaborating in this project and observing the influence of the new toolbox on the company architecture and efficiency of its processes.

6 Conclusion and Future Research

This study presented a reference architecture for a service provision initiative. The architecture helps production machine manufacturers offering an accompanying service to their customers when selling their products, aiming to gain competitive advantages against their rivals and increase customer satisfaction and profit. The proposed target model connects all production steps using real-time data management and analysis, and a dynamic decision-making system. It also reduces the direct interaction of humans with the production process and, subsequently, human errors in disruption and system management.

Further research is needed to go into more detail in analysing the effect of receiving such a service on the operators of the production machines and their reactions to these changes. Moreover, it is required to understand how the real-time data collection process in manual workshops should be done and also the way the changes in the production plan using the dynamic decision-making system should be conveyed to the operators. Moreover, further research is required to go into the technical side of the design and development of the decision-making software and the needed hardware to increase the efficiency of the whole system.

References

1. Homayounfard, A., Zaefarian, G.: Key challenges and opportunities of service innovation processes in technology supplier-service provider partnerships. J. Bus. Res. **139**, 1284–1302 (2022). https://doi.org/10.1016/J.JBUSRES.2021.09.069
2. Ayala, N.F., Gaiardelli, P., Pezzotta, G., le Dain, M.A., Frank, A.G.: Adopting service suppliers for servitisation: which type of supplier involvement is more effective? J. Manuf. Technol. Manag. **32**, 977–993 (2021). https://doi.org/10.1108/JMTM-09-2020-0374/FULL/PDF

3. Biemans, W., Griffin, A.: Innovation practices of B2B manufacturers and service providers: are they really different? Ind. Mark. Manage. **75**, 112–124 (2018). https://doi.org/10.1016/J. INDMARMAN.2018.04.008

4. Aste, N., Manfren, M., Marenzi, G.: Building automation and control systems and performance optimization: a framework for analysis. Renew. Sustain. Energy Rev. **75**, 313–330 (2017). https://doi.org/10.1016/J.RSER.2016.10.072

5. Fargnoli, M., Costantino, F., di Gravio, G., Tronci, M.: Product service-systems implementation: a customized framework to enhance sustainability and customer satisfaction. J. Clean Prod. **188**, 387–401 (2018). https://doi.org/10.1016/J.JCLEPRO.2018.03.315

6. Shokouhyar, S., Shokoohyar, S., Safari, S.: Research on the influence of after-sales service quality factors on customer satisfaction. J. Retail. Consum. Serv. **56**, 102139 (2020). https:// doi.org/10.1016/J.JRETCONSER.2020.102139

7. Rau, C., Zbiek, A., Jonas, J.M.: Creating Competitive Advantage from Services: A Design Thinking Case Study from the Commodities IndustryService design thinking can provide the tools to help companies design value propositions that meet customer needs and sustain competitive advantage. Res. Technol. Manage. **60**, 48–56 (2017). https://doi.org/10.1080/089 56308.2017.1301003

8. Eldor, L.: How collective engagement creates competitive advantage for organizations: a business-level model of shared vision, competitive intensity, and service performance. J. Manage. Stud. **57**, 177–209 (2020). https://doi.org/10.1111/JOMS.12438

9. Pooser, D.M., Browne, M.J.: The effects of customer satisfaction on company profitability: evidence from the property and casualty insurance industry, risk management and insurance. Review **21**, 289–308 (2018). https://doi.org/10.1111/RMIR.12105

10. de Mendonca, T.R., Zhou, Y.: Environmental performance, customer satisfaction, and profitability: a study among large U.S. companies. Sustainability **11**, 5418 (2019). https://doi.org/ 10.3390/SU11195418

11. Javanmardi, A., Alireza Abbasian-Hosseini, S., Liu, M., Hsiang, S.M.: Benefit of cooperation among subcontractors in performing high-reliable planning. Ascelibrary.Org (2017). https:// doi.org/10.1061/(ASCE)ME.1943-5479.0000578

12. Bank, L., et al.: Comparison of simulation-based and optimization-based energy flexible production planning. Procedia CIRP **81**, 294–299 (2019). https://doi.org/10.1016/J.PROCIR. 2019.03.051

13. Lima, R.M., Sousa, R.M.: Agent based prototype for interoperation of production planning and control and manufacturing automation. In: IEEE International Conference on Emerging Technologies and Factory Automation (ETFA), pp. 1225–1232 (2007). https://doi.org/10. 1109/EFTA.2007.4416921

14. Ollinger, L., Schlick, J., Hodek, S.: Leveraging the agility of manufacturing chains by combining process-oriented production planning and service-oriented manufacturing automation. IFAC Proc. Vol. **44**, 5231–5236 (2011). https://doi.org/10.3182/20110828-6-IT-1002.01834

15. Boucharas, V., van Steenbergen, M., Jansen, S., Brinkkemper, S.: The contribution of enterprise architecture to the achievement of organizational goals: a review of the evidence. In: Proper, E., Lankhorst, M.M., Schönherr, M., Barjis, J., Overbeek, S. (eds.) TEAR 2010. LNBIP, vol. 70, pp. 1–15. Springer, Heidelberg (2010). https://doi.org/10.1007/978-3-642-16819-2_1

16. Franck, T., Iacob, M.-E., van Sinderen, M., Wombacher, A.: Towards an integrated architecture model of smart manufacturing enterprises. In: Shishkov, B. (ed.) BMSD 2017. LNBIP, vol. 309, pp. 112–133. Springer, Cham (2018). https://doi.org/10.1007/978-3-319-78428-1_6

17. Kruchten, P.: The Rational Unified Process: An Introduction. Addison-Wesley Professional (2004)

18. Nakagawa, E.Y., Oliveira Antonino, P., Becker, M.: Reference architecture and product line architecture: A subtle but critical difference. In: Crnkovic, I., Gruhn, V., Book, M. (eds.) ECSA 2011. LNCS, vol. 6903, pp. 207–211. Springer, Heidelberg (2011). https://doi.org/10.1007/978-3-642-23798-0_22

19. Peffers, K., Tuunanen, T., Rothenberger, M.A., Chatterjee, S.: A design science research methodology for information systems research. J. Manag. Inf. Syst. **24**, 45–77 (2007). https://doi.org/10.2753/MIS0742-1222240302

20. Baines, T., Ziaee Bigdeli, A., Bustinza, O.F., Shi, V.G., Baldwin, J., Ridgway, K.: Servitization: revisiting the state-of-the-art and research priorities. Int. J. Oper. Prod. Manage. **37**, 256–278 (2017). https://doi.org/10.1108/IJOPM-06-2015-0312/FULL/PDF

21. Gebauer, H., Ren, G.J., Valtakoski, A., Reynoso, J.: Service-driven manufacturing: provision, evolution and financial impact of services in industrial firms. J. Serv. Manag. **23**, 120–136 (2012). https://doi.org/10.1108/09564231211209005/FULL/PDF

22. Kohtamäki, M., Partanen, J., Parida, V., Wincent, J.: Non-linear relationship between industrial service offering and sales growth: the moderating role of network capabilities. Ind. Mark. Manage. **42**, 1374–1385 (2013). https://doi.org/10.1016/J.INDMARMAN.2013.07.018

23. Opresnik, D., Taisch, M.: The manufacturer's value chain as a service - the case of remanufacturing. J. Remanufact. **5**(1), 1–23 (2015). https://doi.org/10.1186/s13243-015-0011-x

24. Tenucci, A., Supino, E.: Exploring the relationship between product-service system and profitability. J. Manage. Gov. **24**(3), 563–585 (2019). https://doi.org/10.1007/s10997-019-09490-0

25. Zhang, Y., Wang, Y., Li, Y.: Facilitating servitization in manufacturing firms: the influence of strategic orientation. Sustain. (Switz.) **13** (2021). https://doi.org/10.3390/SU132413541

26. Iacob, M.E., van Sinderen, M.J., Steenwijk, M., Verkroost, P.: Towards a reference architecture for fuel-based carbon management systems in the logistics industry. Inf. Syst. Front. **15**(5), 725–745 (2013). https://doi.org/10.1007/s10796-013-9416-y

27. Hernández, J.E., Lyons, A.C., Poler, R., Mula, J., Goncalves, R.: A reference architecture for the collaborative planning modelling process in multi-tier supply chain networks: a Zachman-based approach. Prod. Plan. Control **25**, 1118–1134 (2014). https://doi.org/10.1080/09537287.2013.808842

28. Aulkemeier, F., Schramm, M., Iacob, M.E., van Hillegersberg, J.: A service-oriented e-commerce reference architecture. J. Theoret. Appl. Electron. Commer. Res. **11**, 26–45 (2016). https://doi.org/10.4067/S0718-18762016000100003

29. Singh, P.M., van Sinderen, M., Wieringa, R.: Reference architecture for integration platforms. In: Proceedings of the 2017 IEEE 21st International Enterprise Distributed Object Computing Conference, EDOC 2017, January 2017, pp. 113–122 (2017). https://doi.org/10.1109/EDOC.2017.24

30. Verdouw, C.N., Robbemond, R.M., Verwaart, T., Wolfert, J., Beulens, A.J.M.: A reference architecture for IoT-based logistic information systems in agri-food supply chains. Enterp. Inf. Syst. **12**, 755–779 (2018). https://doi.org/10.1080/17517575.2015.1072643

31. Iacob, M.E., Charismadiptya, G., van Sinderen, M., Piest, J.P.S.: An architecture for situation-aware smart logistics. In: Proceedings of the IEEE International Enterprise Distributed Object Computing Workshop, EDOCW, 2019-October, pp. 108–117 (2019). https://doi.org/10.1109/EDOCW.2019.00030

32. Koot, M., Iacob, M.-E., Mes, M.R.K.: A reference architecture for IoT-enabled dynamic planning in smart logistics. In: La Rosa, M., Sadiq, S., Teniente, E. (eds.) CAiSE 2021. LNCS, vol. 12751, pp. 551–565. Springer, Cham (2021). https://doi.org/10.1007/978-3-030-79382-1_33

33. ArchiMate® 3.1 Specification, (n.d.). https://pubs.opengroup.org/architecture/archimate3-doc/. Accessed 19 May 2022

34. Roach, T., Low, G., D'Ambra, J.: Aligning business motivations in a services computing design. Inf. Syst. Dev. Asian Exp., 319–330 (2011). https://doi.org/10.1007/978-1-4419-7355-9_27
35. Ross, J.W., Weill, P., Robertson, D.: Enterprise Architecture as Strategy: Creating a Foundation for Business Execution. Harvard Business Press (2006)
36. Merrifield, R., Calhoun, J., Stevens, D.: The next revolution in productivity. Harv. Bus. Rev. **86**, 72 (2008)
37. Roach, T., Low, G., D'Ambra, J.: CAPSICUM a conceptual model for service oriented architecture. In: 2008 IEEE Congress on Services-Part I, pp. 415–422. IEEE (2008)
38. Silva, H.D., Soares, A.L., Bettoni, A., Francesco, A.B., Albertario, S.: A digital platform architecture to support multi-dimensional surplus capacity sharing. In: Camarinha-Matos, L.M., Afsarmanesh, H., Antonelli, D. (eds.) PRO-VE 2019. IAICT, vol. 568, pp. 323–334. Springer, Cham (2019). https://doi.org/10.1007/978-3-030-28464-0_28
39. Kroh, J., Luetjen, H., Globocnik, D., Schultz, C.: Use and efficacy of information technology in innovation processes: the specific role of servitization. J. Prod. Innov. Manag. **35**, 720–741 (2018). https://doi.org/10.1111/JPIM.12445
40. Singh, M., Jiao, J., Klobasa, M., Frietsch, R.: Servitization of energy sector: emerging service business models and startup's participation. Energies (Basel). **15**, 2705 (2022). https://doi.org/10.3390/EN15072705
41. Shin, J., Kim, Y.J., Jung, S., Kim, C.: Product and service innovation: comparison between performance and efficiency. J. Innov. Knowl. **7**, 100191 (2022). https://doi.org/10.1016/J.JIK.2022.100191
42. Sikora, E., Tenbergen, B., Pohl, K.: Industry needs and research directions in requirements engineering for embedded systems. Requirements Eng. **17**, 57–78 (2012). https://doi.org/10.1007/S00766-011-0144-X/FIGURES/22
43. Bhosale, K.C., Pawar, P.J.: Material flow optimisation of production planning and scheduling problem in flexible manufacturing system by real coded genetic algorithm (RCGA). Flex. Serv. Manuf. J. **31**(2), 381–423 (2018). https://doi.org/10.1007/s10696-018-9310-5
44. Yusuf, L.A., Popoola, K., Musa, H.: A review of energy consumption and minimisation strategies of machine tools in manufacturing process. Int. J. Sustain. Eng. **14**, 1826–1842 (2021). https://doi.org/10.1080/19397038.2021.1964633
45. Bigdeli, A.Z., Kapoor, K., Schroeder, A., Omidvar, O.: Exploring the root causes of servitization challenges: an organisational boundary perspective. Int. J. Oper. Prod. Manage. **41**, 547–573 (2021). https://doi.org/10.1108/IJOPM-08-2020-0507
46. Batlles-delaFuente, A., Belmonte-Ureña, L.J., Plaza-Úbeda, J.A., Abad-Segura, E.: Sustainable business model in the product-service system: analysis of global research and associated EU legislation. Int. J. Environ. Res. Public Health **18** (2021). https://doi.org/10.3390/IJERPH181910123
47. Feng, L., Jiang, R., Ma, C.: Bai, Servitization strategy, manufacturing organizations and firm performance: a theoretical framework. J. Bus. Ind. Market. **36**, 1909–1928 (2021). https://doi.org/10.1108/JBIM-04-2020-0184
48. Huikkola, T., Kohtamäki, M., Ylimäki, J.: Becoming a smart solution provider: reconfiguring a product manufacturer's strategic capabilities and processes to facilitate business model innovation. Technovation (2022). https://doi.org/10.1016/J.TECHNOVATION.2022.102498
49. Ding, J., Wang, M., Zeng, X., Qu, W., Vassiliadis, V.S.: Mass personalization strategy under Industrial Internet of Things: a case study on furniture production. Adv. Eng. Inform. **50** (2021). https://doi.org/10.1016/J.AEI.2021.101439
50. Mourtzis, N., Boli, E., Xanthakis, K.: Alexopoulos, energy trade market effect on production scheduling: an industrial product-service system (IPSS) approach. Int. J. Comput. Integr. Manuf. **34**, 76–94 (2021). https://doi.org/10.1080/0951192X.2020.1858505

51. Ding, K., Jiang, P., Zheng, M.: Environmental and economic sustainability-aware resource service scheduling for industrial product service systems. J. Intell. Manuf. **28**(6), 1303–1316 (2015). https://doi.org/10.1007/s10845-015-1051-7
52. Kassahun, A., Hartog, R.J.M., Tekinerdogan, B.: Realizing chain-wide transparency in meat supply chains based on global standards and a reference architecture. Comput. Electron. Agric. **123**, 275–291 (2016). https://doi.org/10.1016/J.COMPAG.2016.03.004

Author Index

C. Griffo et al. (Eds.): EEWC 2022, LNBIP 473, p. 139, 2023.
https://doi.org/10.1007/978-3-031-34175-5

Printed in the United States
by Baker & Taylor Publisher Services